SOME ASPECTS OF INDONESIAN POLITICS UNDER THE JAPANESE OCCUPATION
1944-1945

BENEDICT R. O'G. ANDERSON

SOME ASPECTS OF INDONESIAN POLITICS UNDER THE JAPANESE OCCUPATION 1944-1945

EQUINOX PUBLISHING (ASIA) PTE LTD
No 3. Shenton Way
#10-05 Shenton House
Singapore 068805

www.EquinoxPublishing.com

Some Aspects of Indonesian Politics
Under the Japanese Occupation:1944-1945
by Benedict R. O'G. Anderson

ISBN 978-602-8397-29-2

First Equinox Edition 2009

Copyright © 1961 by Cornell Southeast Asia Program; renewed 2009.
This is a reprint edition authorized by the original publisher.

Printed in the United States

1 3 5 7 9 10 8 6 4 2

Cornell Modern Indonesia Project Interim Reports

This title was originally published as an "Interim Report" in the Cornell Modern Indonesia Project (CMIP) series organized by the Cornell Southeast Asia Program. CMIP's first "Interim Report" appeared in 1956, during an era when little scholarship on Indonesia was available, and those studies that did appear often lagged far behind the actual events taking place in the country. George Kahin, director of CMIP at the time, explained in his foreword to the first "Interim Report" that these books were intended to address this lack of timely scholarship and encourage lively critical exchanges among researchers and readers. Therefore, as he explained, the "Interim Reports" would be "explicitly tentative and provisional in character." We believe that an understanding of this historical context is key to a full appreciation of these contributions to the study of Indonesia in the twentieth century.

All rights reserved. No part of this publication may be reproduced, stored in a retrieval system, or transmitted in any form or by any means, electronic, mechanical, photocopying, recording or otherwise without the prior permission of Equinox Publishing.

TABLE OF CONTENTS

PREFACE		7
FOREWORD		9
ACKNOWLEDGMENTS		11
INTRODUCTION		13
I.	JAPANESE POLICIES AND PERSPECTIVES	15
II.	CONSEQUENCES OF THE KOISO DECLARATION	23
III.	CHANGING JAPANESE POLICIES, JUNE-JULY 1945	49
IV.	YOUTH GROUPS, ILLEGAL GROUPS AND THE MASSES, TO THE SURRENDER	59
V.	SAIGON	79
VI.	THE INDEPENDENCE PROCLAMATION	85
VII.	ALLIED STRATEGY AND THE PROBLEM OF EXPECTATIONS	111
	Realities.	111
	Illusions, Plans, Stratagems	
	a) The Japanese	117
	b) The Indonesians	123
VIII.	THE FINAL CONFLICT WITH THE JAPANESE AND THE BEGINNINGS OF NEW REGIME	131

PREFACE

The Indonesian revolution, its origins, the course of its development, and its relation to current conditions in Indonesian society has always been a subject of major concern to the Cornell Modern Indonesia Project. Among the principal gaps in the coverage of its history (where both Indonesian and other Asian and Western scholars have given relatively little attention) are the background provided by the final year of Japanese occupation and an account of the first few months of independence, a critical time in which the revolutionary forces acquired their first institutional form.

It is a matter of great regret that most of those Indonesians best qualified to write about this period have had little opportunity for doing so because of their preoccupation with governmental administration and other heavy duties. In the past decade, during which research on Indonesia has taken root at Cornell University, there has been only one substantial study relating to this period, Professor Harry J. Benda's doctoral dissertation, later published under the title of *The Crescent and the Rising Sun*. (The only other significant studies in English, Dr. M. A. Aziz's *Japan's Colonialism and Indonesia* and Professor W. H. Elsbree's *Japan's Role in Southeast Asian Nationalist Movements, 1940-1945* were written without access to the substantial body of documents available to Dr. Benda and Mr. Anderson in Cornell University Library's collection on the Japanese occupation of Indonesia.) Subsequently, a study of outstanding importance has appeared in Japan, *Indoneshia ni okeru Nippon gunsei no kenkyu* (A Study of the Effects of the Japanese Military Occupation on Indonesia) by Shigetada Nishijima, Koichi Kishi, et al.; but, unfortunately, this exists only in the Japanese language and has not as yet been translated into English or Indonesian.

Mr. Benedict Anderson, a member of the Cornell Southeast Asia Program's Modern Indonesia Project and for two years chief teaching assistant in the University's Department of Government, is currently on his way to Indonesia to undertake research concerning the revolutionary period (1945-1949). It is my hope and expectation that as a consequence he will be able to explore the history of the period in a balanced and scholarly way. I believe that the quality of his work in this present Interim Report, one based only on resources available at Cornell, is a substantial earnest of his capacity for doing so.

Mr. Anderson's present study deals with the earliest period of the broader study which he envisages. He wishes it emphasized that the account offered here is an interim report, not a completed mono-graph. It represents his preliminary research, based on the incomplete sources available to him at Cornell. Many of his data are regarded by him as tentative and subject to confirmation or revision — depending upon the information which he encounters during his research in Indonesia. So that this study may be improved, he and I hope that he may secure the cooperation and the full, candid criticism of knowledgeable Indonesian scholars and officials.

Ithaca, New York　　　　　　　　　　　　　　　　George McT. Kahin
September 29, 1961　　　　　　　　　　　　　　　Director

FOREWORD

The central problem with which this study is concerned is the birth of the new Indonesian State out of the debris of Japan's collapsing military Empire. It is a subject of inexhaustible richness and complexity; doubtless many years will pass before a truly all-embracing and understanding account is written. The present study is intended only as a modest, preliminary exploration. The writer hopes that in the course of his research in Indonesia, he will be able to come to a deeper and larger comprehension of this important period in modern Indonesian history.

The main purpose of the study has been to draw together the written documentary materials available in America (particularly at Cornell University), and so present the fullest possible record of the period under consideration. There is some information included which is hardly to be distinguished from hearsay and conjecture; there are serious gaps in the narrative of which the writer is deeply aware. Both have probably distorted this study's picture of the realities of Indonesia's history in the last year of the Occupation. The writer's excuse is that he was concerned to present and juxtapose the perspectives and recollections of as many of the participants as possible — Indonesians, Japanese and Westerners. Though many of their accounts are, for different reasons, one-sided, they illuminate their authors' psychologies and ideological outlooks, and one hopes that from their confrontation, something nearer the truth will emerge. The reader is also asked to bear in mind that many previous accounts of the period here discussed have, perhaps unavoidably, omitted an extensive analysis of the motives and policies of the Japanese Armed Forces, and that therefore, if the Japanese seem to loom large in the framework of this study, it is because an effort has been made to compensate for this omission. A further distortion arises from the fact that the bulk of the materials available to the writer are concerned with conditions in Java and particularly in Djakarta. An undue emphasis has therefore indubitably been laid on developments at the Centre. It is hoped that the reader will make allowances for this bias.

Ithaca, New York   Benedict R. O'G. Anderson
June 30, 1961

ACKNOWLEDGMENTS

The writer would like to take the opportunity to express his deep gratitude for the advice, encouragement and criticism of Professor Kahin, to whom he owes so much besides. He would also like to record his good fortune in having had many talks with Herbert Feith, which have done much to enlarge his own understanding of Indonesian life and politics, On the more strictly scholarly level, the writer acknowledges his great debt to the writings of Professor Kahin and Professor Benda on the Japanese Occupation and the Indonesian Revolution; without the guidance of their work, this study would have been inconceivable. Finally, many thanks are due to John Smail for his detailed criticism of the completed manuscript, and many invaluable suggestions for correcting and improving the text.

INTRODUCTION

There are many problems that confront anyone trying to assess the meaning of the later stages of the Japanese Occupation of Indonesia, as they have been recorded by those who participated in them. There is the serious difficulty of distinguishing between rival claims to the triumphs and glories of the Revolution: the Declaration of Independence, the building of the new state, and the generation of the Revolutionary Spirit. In the records that they have left us, the Japanese, the senior Indonesian nationalist leadership, and the "youth groups" have each claimed pre-eminence for their own roles. Natural ambition and love of glory would in any case impel those participating in the birth of a revolution to emphasize their own share in its conception. But unluckily, many of the accounts that we have were also written at a time when political rivalries and discord had reached a point where the temptation was strong not simply to embellish one's own past, but to blacken that of others. The Japanese, for obvious reasons, were unwilling, in the early years after the war, to reveal very much of their activities under the occupation. It is only in the last few years that they have advanced their claims at all, though certain Dutchmen had long been willing to assign them a major role in the germination of the revolution, sometimes even beyond their due.

CHAPTER ONE
JAPANESE POLICIES AND PERSPECTIVES

On September 7, 1944, the Japanese Premier Kuniaki Koiso announced before a special session of the 85th Imperial Diet that the 'East Indies' would be given independence "in the near future."[1] Instructions issued simultaneously from Tokyo to local commanders in the area specified that the date of Independence should be kept indefinite, and that though the use of nationalist symbols might be encouraged, there was to be no official creation of any Committee for the Preparation of Independence.[2]

The reasons for this Declaration are not hard to find. In July 1944 the strategic island of Saipan had fallen to the Americans. This meant the collapse of the defence line of the Marianas, and the likelihood that the Philippines would be the next target of the enemy. Once the Philippines fell, the lines of sea communication between Tokyo and Indonesia would finally be broken. Not only would the Home Front be deprived of supplies of Indonesian oil, but the defence of the islands would have to be carried on without appreciable help from Tokyo or the mainland. There is good reason to believe that until very late in 1945, the Japanese viewed Java and Sumatra as being the battleground for one of the last great campaigns of the war. But for the defence of the two islands to be truly effective, two conditions would have to be fulfilled. The Southern Fleet would have to remain in Indonesian waters near its oil supply bases (indeed they were forced to do just this by the Battle of Leyte Gulf in October 1944) and the Army would have to assure itself of a basically friendly

---

1 *Kan Po*, #51, pp. 15f. In Indonesian the phrase is '*di kemudian hari*.'
2 Shigetada Nishijima, Koichiro Kishi, *et al.*, *Indoneshia ni okeru Nippon gunsei no kenkyu* (Study of the Effects of the Japanese Military Occupation of Indonesia), Okuma Foundation for Studies in the Social Sciences, Waseda University, Tokyo, 1959, p. 409.

and co-operative population. To fight a war on two fronts against Allied invaders and hostile Indonesians would be very difficult. It is therefore reasonable to say that though many individual Japanese were personally in favour of Indonesian independence, in the minds of the key decision-makers in Tokyo, the reasons for encouraging Indonesian nationalism were primarily strategic.

However a number of factors threatened the success of this policy from the outset. Perhaps the most crucial was the basic cleavage between the Japanese Army and Navy. This cleavage was an old one, and its consequences were felt throughout the Japanese Empire. Essentially the conflicts between the two military bureaucracies had four major aspects: jurisdiction, strategy, personnel and ideology. It appears that in the Imperial Staff's original plans Indonesia had been put in its entirety under the control of the Navy, The area was seen as the strategic supply base for the whole Southern front, and the Navy was to have borne the main responsibility for organizing the commissariat for that front. However the Naval representative on the General Staff objected to this on the ground that they could not cope with such administrative burdens with their limited personnel. In the end, they were assigned only the oil-producing areas of Eastern Indonesia, which at that early stage of the war were vital for the supply of the armies operating in New Guinea, the Solomons, etc.[3] As a result Indonesia was divided administratively between two rival bureau-cracies. When the Army decided for strategic purposes to split its territory into a Java and a Sumatra-Malaya command, the jurisdictional problem became even more awkward. In addition, the Naval Territory was a deficit area for many kinds of vital supplies, including food, textiles, etc. To secure the smooth flow of such supplies from Java to the Naval Territory, and also to help reduce friction between the two services, Rear-Admiral Maeda was appointed at his own suggestion, to the liaison office of Naval Attaché in Djakarta. It was from this strategic position that the Admiral was to play the decisive role in the transfer of power from Japanese to Indonesian hands that we shall be examining later.

---

3 There is a report that Admiral Maeda, then on the Navy's General Staff in Tokyo, argued against this arrangement, significantly on the ground that it would allow the Army to set up two little kingdoms of its own.

The strategic viewpoints of the two services were also in sharp conflict. The Army had been traditionally oriented towards the Continent. It had Korea, Manchuria and Northern China as its primary targets. It saw its chief enemies as being Russia, and to a lesser degree China. Its interests in the territories it controlled were primarily strategic and exploitative. Manchuria and Korea, for example, were considered first as buffer states between Japan and the two major continental powers, and secondly as important industrial bases for the supply of the Army and the Japanese homeland. The Army's administrative policies were not unlike those of European colonialism, though the external forms were somewhat different. A puppet regime, for example, was generally installed under the scarcely veiled control of the Japanese Armed Forces. By contrast, Naval strategy was oriented eastwards and southwards. The Navy's history and traditions had led it to have much closer dealings with the (essentially Naval) Anglo-Saxon powers than the Army ever had. A good many Japanese Naval officers had been trained in Britain.[4] It was the relatively rare Japanese Army officer who did a tour of foreign duty outside France or Germany.[5] The struggle in the early thirties over the ratio between the naval strengths of America, Britain and Japan had aroused considerable nationalist indignation in Japan, and nowhere more so than in Army circles.[6] But this indignation was aroused primarily by the symbolic humiliation of Japan implied in her naval inferiority to the Western powers, much less by the concrete military implications of the system. The Japanese Navy however derived from the struggle to alter the ratio a fairly shrewd estimate of the probable risks involved in any

---

4 Cf. E. Brunsveld van Hulten, Military Auditor, *Rapport over de Japansche Invloede op de Merdekabeweging en de Gebeurtenissen in de Augustdagen*, after the preliminary interrogation of Japanese prisoners in Singapore, July 17-24, 1946, p. 2. These and other *Statements* cited hereafter are taken from a collection of documents made by Mr. Shigetada Nishijima from the archives of the Rijksinstituut voor Oorlogsdocumentatie at Amsterdam. They form part of a mass of data on the Japanese occupation accumulated through Dutch interrogations of Japanese prisoners-of-war in 1946-1947. Hitherto little systematic use has been made of these materials in English, the exceptions being the studies by Aziz and Elsbree cited below.
5 However General Nishimura, of whom more below, lived in the United States from February 1936 to March 1938. He studied the English language in Boston and American military tactics in Washington. See his *Statement* of June 6, 1946, under interrogation at Changi prison in Singapore, p. 1.
6 Cf. e. g. Hugh Byas, *Government by Assassination*, Alfred A. Knopf, New York, 1942, pp. 44-46.

conflict with the other two world naval powers.⁷ From the time of Pearl Harbor onwards, the Army and Navy found themselves increasingly at odds, the Navy considering the Army's tendency to overcommit its forces and overextend its lines of communication sheer stupidity, and the Army convinced of the Navy's 'Anglo-Saxon-mindedness' and timidity in support of the Army's plans. This hostility became especially marked after the fall of Saipan. The Army was bitter at the Navy's supposed lack of support, while the Navy claimed that it was being destroyed piecemeal by the Americans because the Army insisted on trying to defend so many different areas simultaneously.⁸

On the level of personnel, the Navy disposed of a far more sophisticated and 'select' staff. It was the elite service into which young cadets usually tried to enrol before reconciling themselves to the more 'popular' Army. As a consequence the Navy had considerably higher social prestige. Moreover the course of naval life permitted a degree of international and cosmopolitan experience that few Army officers could match.⁹ There was therefore a natural tendency towards a Navy superiority complex, which in turn often generated Army suspicions and resentments. Generally speaking, the two services were united only in the face of civilian interference in what they regarded as 'military' affairs.¹⁰

---

7 Cf. F. C. Jones, *Japan's New Order in East Asia 1937-1945*, Oxford University Press, London, 1954, pp. 104, 115-119, 191-192 and 222, for the attitude of Admiral Yonai as Navy spokesman, first as Navy Minister and then as Premier.
8 This feeling apparently percolated right down the military hierarchy. Cf. Anonymous Japanese Officer, *Beschouwingen ouer de algemene en financiele voorbereiding van der Indonesische Onafhankelijkheids-beweging door de Japaners*, June 21-23, 1947, p. 24.
9 Admiral Maeda, for example had been for some time in Indonesia before the war. He had also served as Naval Attaché in Berlin, and later in Amsterdam when the Nazi Armies occupied the Netherlands. Cf. E. B. van Hulten, *Rapport., op. cit.*, July 24, 1946, p. 1.
10 Civilian opposition to the military generally centred in the Foreign Ministry and the Ministry for Greater East Asia. Both were supposed to have a hand in policy-making for Indonesia, but in wartime Japan their influence was limited. Generally they were more liberally disposed towards Indonesia, essentially for diplomatic and political reasons. It was on them that the pressure of Allied promises, such as the Atlantic Charter, was most powerfully felt. However it is interesting to note that one observer believes that the Koiso Declaration itself represented a defection of the Army to the two civilian ministries. The reason for this break in military solidarity seems to have been the Army's anxiety (in Tokyo at least) for a secure local base for their more isolated units, in view of the pre-cariousness of communications between Japan and South East Asia. Cf. R. Soerjono Wirjodiatmodjo, *Die Besatzungzeit (vom 9 Maerz '42 bis 17 August '45)*, unpublished mimeo, 1959, pp, 30, 34. See also Jones, *op. cit., passim.*, and *Statement* of Major Tadakazu Ishizima, Intelligence Officer attached to Army HQ at Saigon and Singapore, dated November 16, 1946, p. 2.

Finally there seems to have been an ideological split in the Armed Forces. This cleavage is far less definite and explicit than the others, and to some extent the lines of division do not run directly between the services. The classic conflict within the Army, between the Young Officers and the Old Guard, had begun as a conflict of classes and generations which took the schematic ideological form of a radical anti-capitalist nationalism opposed to a conservative, capitalistic imperialism. A great many of the younger officers in the Army came from depressed rural areas, either from peasant or déclassé samurai families. A combination of circumstances, notably the World Depression, the contraction of Japanese world markets, the policies of the older colonial powers in the Far East, and certain well-established authoritarian Japanese traditions, molded them into a new elite without a genuinely functional position in a modern industrial society such as early twentieth century Japan. The centralization of power in Japanese society and the extremes of oligarchy in the government created a ruling class with a dangerously narrow base. Between the top civilian administrators, the Zaibatsu and the ruling military cliques of the Satsuma and Choshu clans, and the increasingly industrialized society they ruled, there was no gradual dispersion of power and social influence. The young officers were conscious of themselves as the elite of a numerically powerful and yet under-privileged provincial rural class. In the circumstances of the twenties and thirties, the enemies of that class were seen as the 'monopoly capitalists', their military allies at the Imperial Court and the foreigners who were plotting to limit the power and thwart the destiny of Japan. The political product of these sociological and psychological forces does not fall neatly into 'left' or 'right' categories. The vague political theories of this new elite called for some form of state 'socialism' and an aggressive 'spirit of national unity' under the quasi-religious leadership of the Emperor: a pattern which clearly foreshadows an important strand in the political thinking of many post-colonial nationalisms. The peculiarity of the Japanese case was that while the 'younger generation's' skills were technical and bureaucratic, as professional soldiers, their vocation was the more 'political' one of symbol-manipulation. In the Army at least, limited educational opportunities, and what has been called the culture-bound nature of Japanese society, tended to give the radicalism of the younger officers a basically xenophobic tinge. Even where they could find elements abroad with an essentially similar outlook, they were rarely able to empathize with those elements. Psychologically, they were in blinkers. To spread their 'word', they could rarely rise above the technique of direct Japanization.[11]

In the Navy however, where some of the same generational and class cleavages existed, a different psychological type seems to have emerged, a type in which the radical xenophobia of the younger Army officers' introverted nationalism was transformed by a wider life experience and education. Their transformed nationalism expressed itself in a genuine if limited form of internationalism. Men like Admiral Shibata and Rear-Admiral Maeda in Indonesia, for example, were able to perceive and empathize with the psychological traits of other Asian nationalisms. The ideology of such men has been described as national-communism, but the description is not wholly apt. Nor perhaps is 'internationalism' alone, with its sense of an all-embracing humanism. The internationalism of these men rarely meant 'love for all men, including Westerners.' It was essentially an ability to find the satisfactions of Japanese nationalism in a feeling of 'common life-experience' vis-a-vis the West, shared with the renascent nationalisms of South East Asia. And in addition there were the more subtle satisfactions enjoyed by any group of 'elite reformers' in guiding the destinies of their less fortunate fellows.

Of course superimposed on these two 'younger generation' groups were the clannish and conservative military cliques left over from the Meiji period, who held the ultimate power. Essentially they were not unlike the typical capitalistic imperialists of the 19th Century, nationalistic, pragmatic, exploitative and fundamentally uninterested in their colonies as such, even for the purposes of 'Japanization.' Their conduct towards countries like Indonesia could be expected to be guided by rational considerations of political and military strategy. They would tend to despise both the 'crudity' of the younger Army, and the 'sentimentality' of the younger Naval officers.[12]

---

11 A good specimen of the type was General Itagaki, Commander of the 7th Army group at Singapore in 1945. He was a well-known member of the *Kodoha* radical group, was involved in the Manchurian incident of 1931, and became Minister for War under Konoye and Hiranuma. He was violently anti-British. See Hillis Lory, *Japan's Military Masters*, Viking Press, 1943, p. 174, and Richard Storry, *The Double Patriots*, Chatto and Windus, 1957, pp. 77-79, 84-85, 92, 229, 244, 254.

12 Cf. Storry, *op. cit.*, especially pp, 126-203, for military factionalism, A typical *Toseiha* or

The inevitable conflicts within and between the two military bureaucracies caused by the factors outlined above, bedevilled the whole question of a coherent 'Indonesia policy.' The problem was further complicated by the enormous extent of Japanese conquests, the lack of good communications in Indonesia (indeed in South East Asia as a whole), and Japanese inexperience in dealing with the area. The Army line of command in South East Asia extended down from the Supreme War Council in Tokyo through Marshal Terauchi's Southern Territories Command at Saigon, General Itagaki's 7th Army Group Headquarters in Singapore to the 25th Army's Headquarters at Bukittinggi in Sumatra, and the 16th Army's Headquarters in Djakarta. The Navy had its own separate line of command running down from the Navy Ministry through the 10th Area Fleet Headquarters in Singapore to the 2nd Fleet's Headquarters in Surabaya and Makassar.[13] Thus the two hierarchies were only co-ordinated at the highest level, though in the last two months of the war, for practical purposes of closer communication, the Navy in Indonesia was put under the orders of Marshal Terauchi.

Two other difficulties faced Tokyo and the occupying Armies in attempting to formulate and execute a coherent Indonesian policy. One was the great heterogeneity of the territories they governed. The level of political sophistication and awareness on Java, for example, was far above that on Kalimantan. The possibilities for advancing political participation in a 'war' area like Sulawesi or the Moluccas were far less than in a 'supply' area like Java, Trained administrators were far more numerous and effective in Java than in any of the Outer Islands. On the other hand 'class differences' in Java were more marked than anywhere else, except possibly in North and East Sumatra, and some parts of Sulawesi, This heterogeneity was decidedly useful so long as the main purpose of military rule was physical control and the extraction of resources. The old colonial formula

---

conservative senior Army officer was Count Hisaichi Terauchi, Commander of the Southern Territories from October 1941 to September 1945, He was Minister for War in the *Toseiha*-dominated Hirota Cabinet formed immediately after the February 1936 Affair. Storry, *op. cit.*, p, 192, Cf, the Anonymous Japanese Officer, Beschouwlngen..., *op. cit.*, p, 16.

13 See *Statement* under Interrogation of Captain Masuzo Yanagihara, Deputy Chief of the Naval Administration Office in Makassar, dated July 6th and 8th, 1946, p. 2. See also *Statement* of General Otoshi Nishimura, Head of the General Affairs Office in Djakarta, under interrogation, Changi prison, Singapore, May 31-June 6, 1946, p, 2,

of divide and rule was used with considerable skill by the Japanese. Islamic, secular nationalist and bureaucratic elites were manipulated against one another. Each group was forced to turn to the Japanese as arbiters to win political decisions in their favour.[14] But once the policy became one of extracting, not physical resources, but intellectual and psychological cooperation, the divisions which the Japanese themselves had fostered worked against them: dissension among the elites was hardly conducive to maximizing Indonesia's contribution to the war effort.

Secondly, there was the problem of administering policy. At the beginning of the occupation, the Army had relied largely on Japanese civilians resident in Indonesia to see that its policies were effectively administered, employing them either as bureaucrats or as spies, or as both. However, from the beginning, it had been found necessary to make use of Indonesian talents. Indonesian administrators found themselves assigned positions much higher than they had been permitted to attain in the Dutch colonial period. The decline of Japanese personnel available for civilian administrative purposes (and the aversion of most military men for civilian administrative work) combined with the new policy of encouraging Indonesian political participation inaugurated after the Koiso Declaration, (which meant, in the absence of a legislature or political parties, a greater share in the bureaucratic decision-making process) created a difficult situation. In the latter stages of the occupation there was a tiny crust of Japanese executives who gave the orders, but who depended on the far greater body of Indonesian administrators to carry them out, and to provide them with the information on which their orders could be based. Here was a subtle block to Japanese policy-making. On the way down the governmental apparatus orders were often imperceptibly transmuted. Anti-imperialist slogans and propaganda tended to drop specific reference to America, Britain and Holland. Pro-Japanese propaganda could often be infused with directly nationalist appeals. And in the flow of information up the bureaucratic structure from the villages to the Japanese military authorities, the scope and intensity of Indonesian 'demands' for independence could be subtly enlarged and deepened.

---

14 See H. Benda, *The Crescent and the Rising Sun*, W. van Hoeve Ltd., The Hague and Bandung, 1958, for a superb analysis of Japanese policy towards the Islamic elite (and incidentally the secular nationalists as well).

CHAPTER TWO
CONSEQUENCES OF THE KOISO DECLARATION

The Koiso Declaration was received with a certain amount of ambivalence in Indonesia. It was obviously designed to encourage the Indonesian leadership to greater and more active co-operation, and to persuade the Indonesian masses that Independence was conditional on their massive support during the coming final struggle for victory in the Pacific Many Indonesian leaders however were aware of the serious military situation. By the middle of 1944, information coming from clandestine radios and from Indonesians working in the Propaganda (Information) Division of the Military Administration, had convinced many that a Japanese defeat was inevitable. Moreover as time wore on, Japanese attempts to explain their admitted retreats as part of a strategy of *'reculer pour mieux sauter'* began to wear thin. But for the time being there was little that the Indonesian leaders could do but work with the Japanese while maintaining a steady pressure for increased autonomy. Both Indonesians and Japanese were naturally out to win the maximum of concessions from their antagonists, in exchange for a minimum of sacrifices on their own part.

The promise of independence contained in the Declaration was vague enough for the silent battle of pressure and counter-pressure to be continued on much the same terms as before. The Indonesian leaders demanded some concrete steps towards fulfilling the promise of independence, and claimed that only increased autonomy could really fire the Indonesian people to make the sacrifices the Japanese demanded. Any delay would simply mean a politically and militarily dangerous disillusionment on the part of the masses. The Japanese authorities of the 16th Army however made it clear for their part that the Indonesians could expect Independence only as a gift (*'hadiah'*) in exchange for genuine and wholehearted co-operation. In the struggle for advantage then, the Indonesians had the psychological benefit of their knowledge of Japan's declining military power, while the Japanese had only their monopoly of the instruments of violence and the promises they held out.

Nevertheless in the six months that followed the Koiso Declaration, the movement towards independence moved forward at a snail's pace. As a sop to the Indonesian elite, the Japanese did, late in December 1944, increase the number of *Sanyos* (Advisors) to the various departments of the Military Administration.[1] These *Sanyos* were assembled into a *Dewan Sanyo* (Council of Advisors)[2] which was supposed to act as a sort of 'Privy Council' to the government. The membership of the *Tyoo Sangi In* (Central Advisory Council)[3] was also increased.[4] A new

---

1 *Kan Po*, # 56, (December 10, 1944), pp. 15f. These included: R. Pandji Soeroso to replace M. Yamin in the General Affairs Department; Mr. R. M. Sartono in the Home Affairs Department (he was replaced in June 1945 by R.A.A. Wiranatakusuma); Ki Hadjar Dewantoro in Education; Dr. Buntaran Martoatmodjo in the Health Department; Mr. R. Pandji Singgih in the Labour Section; Dr, Samsi Sastrawidagda in the Finance Department; Oto Iskandardinata in the Department of Public Security; Soekardjo Wirjopranoto in Propaganda; Abikoesno Tjokrosoejoso in the Public Works Section.
2 *Kan Po*, # 55, (November 23, 1944), p. 6. (*Makloemat Gunseikan* # 68).
3 Henceforth referred to as C.A.C.
4 For the announcement of this body's creation, see *Kan Po*, #24 (August 10, 1943), pp. 10f. In many respects the C.A.C. was not unlike the pre-war Volksraad, except that it was not even allowed to criticize the regime as the Volksraad had done. It had no legislative powers whatever. It was supposed to act as a purely advisory body, answering 'questions' put to it by the military government. It seems to have been quite ineffective for most of its life, though Japanese protests that it was imagining itself to be a 'Parliamentary body' indicate that its ineffectiveness was not of its members' making. As of its Seventh Session, the C.A.C. 's membership was as follows;
Members appointed by the Government:

K. H. Abdul Halim
Ki Hadjar Dewantoro
Drs. Mohammad Hatta
Ki Bagoes Hadikoesoemo
Liem Thwan Tik
Oei Tiang Tjoei
Dr. Abdul Rasjid
Dr. Samsi Sastrawidagda
Mr. R. M. Sartono
Ir. Soekarno
R. Pandji Soeroso
K. R. M. T. Ario Woerjaningrat
R. Gatot Mangkupradja
Mr. R. Soedjono
*Abdurahman Baswedan
*Mr. Mohammad Djamin
*Mr. Johannes Latuharhary

Br. R. Boentaran Martoatmodjo
Prof. Dr. P. Ario Hoesein Djajadiningrat

Oto Iskandardinata
R. M. A. A. Koesoemo Oetojo
K. H. M. Mansoer
Oey Tjong Hauw
R. Roeslan Wongsokoesoemo
Mr. R. Samsoedin
R. Soekardjo Wirjopranoto
Bendoro P. Ario Soerjodiningrat
K. H. Abdoel Wachid Hasjim
R. Abikoesno Tjokrosoejoso
R. M. Margono Djojohadikoesoemo
Mr. R. M. Soemanang
*P. F. Dahler
*Mas Goenari

provincial administrative post was also created, the Vice-Resident (*Huku Syuutyookan*) which was usually filled by an Indonesian, generally an experienced *prijaji* civil servant.[5] The Residents however remained Japanese in all but three residencies. There is some reason to believe that these moves were designed to strengthen the hands of the *prijaji*, who had simply their administrative skills and institutional power, vis-à-vis the secular nationalist and Islamic elites who had more 'popular' bases of influence. The Japanese probably hoped in this way to provide channels

*Ir. R. Oekar Bratakoesoema	*Mr. Alexander A. Maramis
*R. Roedjito	*R. Prawoto Soemodilogo
*Mr. Muhammad Yamin	*R. Wiwoho Poerbohadidjojo
*Drs. Yap Tjwan B ing	

Members elected from Advisory Councils in the Residencies and Djakarta Raya:

R. Z. Soeriakartalegawa (Banten)	R. Ibrahim Singadilaga (Djakarta)
Ir. M. A. Sofwan (Djakarta Raya)	Dr. Marzoeki Mahdi (Bogor)
M. Soetisna Sendjaja (Priangan)	Dr. Mohamad Toha (Tjirebon)
Dr. Maas (Pekalongan)	Dr. Sardjito Kartomihardjo (Kedu)
R. Sardjono Danoedibroto (Banjumas)	
Mr. R. Soejoedi (Semarang)	Bandoro P. Ario Poeroebojo (Jogjakarta)
R. Mas Aris (Pati)	
K. R. T. R. Wediodiningrat (Madiun)	Drs. K. R. M. T. Adipati
Mr. R. Soenarko (Malang)	Sosrodiningrat (Solo)
R.A.A. Soerjonegoro (Madura)	R. H. Fatchoerrahman (Bodjonegoro)
Poero Martodipoero (Kediri)	*R, Soedirman (Surabaja)
	*Asmo Asmodisastro (Besuki)

Those names marked with a star are the new members. Cf. *Djawa Baroe*, I, #21, (November 1,1943), pp. 4f;II, #18, (September 15, 1944), p. 29; III, #6, (March 15, 1945), p. 4. Also Asia Raya, November 13, 1944, February 12, 1945, and June 15 and 19, 1945. See also John O. Sutter, *Indonesianisasi, Politics in a Changing Economy, 1940-1955*, Data Paper No. 36, Southeast Asia Program, Department of Far Eastern Studies, Cornell University, Ithaca, N. Y., 1959, Appendix B, pp. 1268f., for further details. *N. B.* On January 3, 1945, a similar body was created in Sumatra, cf. *Pandji Poestaka*, 23, # 2, (February 1945), p. 58.

5 These appointments included initially:
Hadji Ahmad Sanoesi (Bogor); R. M. A. A. Soeriatanoedibrata (Tjirebon)
R. T. A. Milono (Pati); Mr. R. P. Iskaq Tjokroadisoerjo (Banjumas)
Mr. K. R. M. T. Wongsonegoro (Semarang); R. Abdoerahirn Pratalykrama (Kediri)
R. Poerardiredjo (Priangan);
Mr. R. S. Budhyarto Martoatmodjo (Madiun).
See *Kan Po*, #56, (Dec. 10, 1944),p. 16, On April23, 1945 three more such appointments were made: R. Soedirman (Surabaja);
R.A.A. Tjakraningrat (Madura); Mr. M, Besar (Pekalongan).
See *Kan Po*, #67, (May 25, 1945), p. 20. Four final appointments were made on June 15, 1945:
R. Rangga Tirtasoejatna (Banten)
R. M. T. A. Koesnandar (Madiun); Mr. R. S. Budhyarto Martoatmodjo (Besuki)
Mr, R. Pandji Singgih (Malang).
See Kan Po, #69, (June 25, 1945), p. 39. Thus by the end of the occupation there were Vice-Residents in every Residence but Djakarta, Kedu and Bodjonegoro, ready to take over the top regional administrative posts, and in these three areas the Residents themselves were now Indonesians.

whereby military directives would have a maximum effectiveness among the mass of Indonesians, and to consolidate a bureaucratic structure to which power could be transferred as slowly or as rapidly as they wished, without any break in governmental authority or any chance for chaos and anarchy to break out. It should also be noted that all the new positions were advisory, carrying no powers with them, except the informal ones created by experience and tactful manoeuvre.

Whereas the Koiso Declaration was apparently received by the masses with some enthusiasm in Sumatra and the Naval Territories,[6] and even in Java, the bureaucratic promotions that followed it were not of any great publicity value and probably pleased only a limited circle of top leaders. These were however needed to mobilize the masses. The deeper significance of the appointments lies however in the fact that they reveal the beginning of a steady progress towards a 'dual apparatus' of government at the highest levels of the administration. This was to be of crucial importance when the Japanese finally 'transferred' power to the Indonesians late in 1945. One might use the simile of the relay race, and say that during the last six months of the occupation, the two bureaucratic directorates ran things side by side until the baton of power was finally relinquished to the Indonesian leadership.

In spite of these liberalizing measures, the Japanese found the Javanese population restless and uneasy. The 16th Army had to bear the brunt of the growing tension and dissatisfaction, as conditions on the Outer Islands were much more placid.[7] Some indications of the changing atmosphere

---

6 Cf. *Statement* of Captain Masuzo Yanagihara, July 6, 8, 1946, p. 4; the rather sour comments of Lt. Gen. Toshio Miyake, Governor of Palembang are also revealing. See his *Statement* (from Changi prison) Dec. 19, 1946, p. 1,

7 Cf. *Statement* of Captain Yanagihara, p. 5, where he discusses the diffi-culties of trying to create a mass movement in the Naval Territory, based on all strata of the population. He adds, somewhat in contradiction to his description of the reception of the Koiso Declaration, that only the wealthy local entrepreneurs were enthusiastic about independence, because they were promised the local assets and 'good will' of Japanese firms operating in the area as soon as independence would be announced.

The situation on Sumatra seems to have been fairly calm too. Yet Major-General Fumie Shimura, head of the Civil Administration on Sumatra from January 1944 to July 1945, personally rejected a proposed 'propaganda' tour in his territory by Soekarno or Hatta, because he felt the repercussions might be undesirable. See his *Statement*, no date, pp. 1 and 5.

It is perhaps worth adding that when the Naval Administration decided to relax its highly repressive anti-nationalist policies after the American landings on Leyte in October 1944, it agreed to invite the two leaders to tour its territories. Asa result Hatta visited Kalimantan and

on Java can be gained from the Peta uprising at Blitar in February 1945 (see below, Chapter III), and the Seventh Session of the C.A.C. The C.A.C. met on February 21st, and inducted its 14 new members. It seems that its discussions were rather more lively than usual. In any case it made a number of instructive 'suggestions' to the Military Government.[8] Of these the most important were:

1. Expansion of military training among the masses.
2. An improvement in the working conditions, the food and the clothing of the Romushas.[9]
3. A relaxation of restrictions on the passage of non-strategic goods from Residency to Residency.
4. The creation of a New Life Movement to prepare the masses for independence "both physically and psychologically."
5. The integration of the Masjumi and the *Djawa Hookookai* by the Military Government, for the sake of national unity. The Council complained that the two had separate organizations "though there is no conflict between them."[10]

Soekarno Sulawesi, Bali and the Lesser Sundas. However there is no indication that these visits had any very significant consequences. Cf. *Statement* of Captain Yanagihara, p. 6. Other aspects of the Navy's 'liberalizing' poli-cies included the expansion of the numbers and the 'powers' of provincial and municipal councils. See *Report # 58*, U.S. Office of Strategic Services, Research and Analysis Branch, Honolulu, February 28, 1945, p. 9.

8 In fact, the suggestions were formally made to the *Saikosikikan*, or Commander-in-Chief of the 16th Army on Java, at that time Lt. Gen. Kumashiki Harada. He held a position somewhat analogous to that of the former Dutch Governor-General, though in practice, on account of his military responsibilities, he had little to do with running the civilian administrative system.

9 The Romushas were forced labourers made use of by the Japanese in mining and construction projects, mainly in Indonesia, Thailand and Burma. They were partly conscripted, partly seduced by promises of high pay and good living conditions, and patriotic propaganda. They were given, ironically, the title of Heroes of Labour. Thousands died or disappeared under the inhuman conditions in which they were compelled to work. For an estimate of the losses, derived from Japanese sources, see Muhammad Abdul Aziz, *Japan's Colonialism and Indonesia*, Martinus Nijhoff, the Hague, 1955, p. 242. His figure is about 200, 000 dead or missing.

10 *Djawa Baroe*, III, # 6, (March 15, 1945), pp. 4f. The *Djawa Hookookai* was an extensive mass-based organization, set up in January 1944 to replace the former *Putera*, which, partly because it was confined to ethnic Indonesians, the Japanese felt was not sufficiently under their control. The new organization had Japanese officials at its command posts, had an extensive village network at its base, and was multi-racial — all in contrast to the *Putera*. Soekarno served as its Secretary-General. Its Indonesian leadership was predominantly 'secular Nationalist.' The Masjumi, founded in October 1943, was an organization designed to merge all pre-existing Islamic groups and organizations. It had an entirely Indonesian executive, enjoyed extensive grass-roots backing, and flourished under the special protection of the Japanese authorities. For a detailed analysis of the

The first of these suggestions promised to benefit both Japanese and Indonesians alike, or at least gave the appearance of doing so. The Japanese steadily refused to train more than a very few Indonesians with real weapons, generally equipping them only with sharpened bamboo spears or imitation wooden rifles. Not unnaturally they were afraid of revolt against their own often oppressive rule. Yet military training was likely to be a good preliminary method of channelling the energies of the masses into the war effort. On the other hand the Indonesian leaders wanted better training for their own people to prepare them for an anticipated fight for independence, whether against the Dutch or the Japanese. The second and third suggestions may have originated from the Indonesians themselves, unprompted by Japanese insistence. The third suggestion is particularly important as it threatened to break down the elaborate plans of the Japanese for regional autarchy. These plans were designed partly to minimize the damage done by the deterioration or destruction of lines of communication and transportation under an enemy attack (and thus to allow local guerilla activities to be carried on as freely as possible), and partly to ensure a more efficient rationing and distribution of available supplies. The scheme also had the advantage of lightening the burden on the very meagre transportation facilities on Java.[11]

The New Life Movement was part of the overall Army policy of doing everything possible to stimulate nationalist sentiment without allowing it to take concrete political expression. The Movement, when established, was ostensibly non-political. Its 'program' consisted of sending important Indonesian leaders into the villages to set examples of thrift, hard work and discipline, and to encourage the more intensive cultivation (for war purposes) of ordinary farm land and the peasants' family plots. It is notable that an unusually non-Japanese set of slogans was provided for these emissaries.

---

role and organization of the Masjumi, see H. Benda, op. cit., Chapter 7. For the *Djawa Hookookai*, cf. Aziz, *op. cit.*, pp. 222-224.

11 See Aziz, *op. cit.*, pp. 185-188. Almost inevitably this artificial autarchic policy tended to break down. For a variety of reasons, including the sheer struggle for survival, wide-spread smuggling operations grew up. In many cases the police and other administrative officers involved in executing the policy found themselves involved in this smuggling, which often acquired a 'patriotic' aspect. The concept of 'patriotic smuggling' for one's people proved popular even after Independence, with of course unfortunate consequences in the changed political circumstances.

In any event, both the major political organizations on Java at the time, the Masjumi and the *Djawa Hookookai*, actively participated in the movement, even competing for its leadership. It is hard to estimate how successful the new movement was, mainly because its goals were almost purely psychological. Some observers claimed that it was a highly efficient way of bringing the secular Nationalist leaders and their Moslem counterparts into closer contact with the villagers. Other reports allege that on the contrary, the 'agricultural' activities of these leaders only lowered their prestige and opened them to ridicule; and that no remarkable rise in village productivity followed the New Life Movement's energetic campaign.

The 16th Army was also careful to ignore the suggestion made by the secular nationalist leaders in the C.A.C., for a merger of the Masjumi and the *Djawa Hookookai*. It can hardly be doubted that this 'suggestion' was a thinly veiled invitation to the Japanese authorities to stop their earlier policy of playing off the Islamic elite against the secular nationalists. If the demand had been accepted it would have meant the absorption of the Masjumi into the secular nationalist-dominated *Hookookai*.[12] The demand therefore faced the Japanese with an awkward dilemma. Their control, as we have seen, rested to an important degree on the formula of divide and rule, which entailed keeping the Moslem elite unabsorbed. Yet a strengthening of the war effort could hardly be expected while the two elites were permitted to devote their energies to their mutual rivalries. On this occasion, by ignoring the secular nationalists' suggestion, the Japanese sided with the Moslem elements. But as one shrewd observer

---

12 The division between secular nationalists and Moslems was paralleled among the youth as well. The *Barisan Pelopor*, set up in September 1944 (see *Pandji Poestaka*, 23, # 17, (September 1, 1944), p. 540), was a youth organization designed to extend the reach and deepen the dynamism of the *Djawa Hookookai*. It was under direct Indonesian leadership, being headed by Soekarno, with Oto Iskandardinata and Dr. Boentaran Martoatmodjo as his executive assistants. Many prominent nationalists were attached to it from all over Java. It was the most heavily indoctrinated of the various Indonesian youth corps, and maintained its anti-Western, authoritarian and fervently nationalist character, when, after the Declaration of Independence, it became the *Barisan Banteng*. It later came under the influence of Tan Malakka. It probably numbered somewhere near 80, 000. See Aziz, *op. cit.*, p. 230, n. 3; Benda, *op. cit.*, p. 178; George McT. Kahin, *Nationalism and Revolution in Indonesia*, Cornell University Press, Ithaca, 1952, p. 163.

To counterbalance the Barisan Pelopor, the Masjumi had its own youth organization, the Hizboe'llah (Army of God), probably numbering about 50, 000. It was given much the same kind of ideological training as its counterpart, though of course with a heavy Islamic colouring as well. Cf. Aziz, loc. cit. and Benda, op. cit. p. 179,

has pointed out, the hesitations of the Japanese did not last long. For the very boldness of the secular nationalists' claim was a clear indication that as the Japanese relinquished gradually their tight grip on Indonesian political life, the "real" strengths of the rival elites they had fostered became increasingly apparent. The rapid sinking of the Masjumi into the background as the year wore on, revealed the comparative poverty of its leadership's political and administrative experience, and the greater 'inclusiveness' of the political philosophy of the secular nationalists.[13] Even if one does not accept this analysis lit its entirety, it is fair to say that within the very heterogenous Masjumi organization, the Japanese encouraged the predominance of 'symbol-manipulating' mass leaders, whom they found they could influence more easily, at the expense of former members of such bodies as the *Jong Islamieten Bond*,[14] who had the administrative skills to compete with the top secular nationalist and *prijaji* leaders.

The increasingly strong nationalist sentiment revealed by the Seventh Session of the C.A.C., in addition to the Blitar revolt (see below), and of course the promises made in the Koiso Declaration, led the 16th Army in February of 1945 to attempt to channel and perhaps divert nationalist aspirations by an apparently significant concession. It decided to create a Committee for the Investigation of Indonesian Independence (*Baden Penjelidik Kemerdekaan Indonesia*).[15] The idea was reportedly poorly received in Singapore and Saigon, but Tokyo approved.[16] A conference of top Japanese administrative officials was convened late in February to work out just when the Committee would be inaugurated and what its precise function would be. However the conference did not prove to be very productive, and we shall see that this was to create considerable difficulties for the Japanese when the Committee eventually met. The

---

13 Benda, *op. cit.*, pp. 177-179.
14 A pre-war association of 'modernist' and highly educated Islamic leaders, including Hadji A goes Salim, Mr. Roem, Dr. Sukiman, Mohammed Natsir, Sardian, etc. They were often at sharp odds with the more traditional and less 'western-educated' Islamic leadership. Interestingly enough however, many of them assumed key positions in the executive of the *Hizboe 'llah*. Cf. *Soeara Moeslimin Indonesia*, III, #2, (January 15, 1945), p. 13, Among those on the *Poesat Pimpinan* (Central Directorate) were Roem, Jusuf Wibisono, Anwar Tjokroa-minoto, Prawoto Mangkoesasmita.
15 Henceforth referred to as B.P.K.I.
16 Nishijima, Kishi, et al., op, cit., p. 417; Wirjodiatmodjo, op. cit., p. 37.

essential idea behind the Committee was to side-track nationalist energy into harmless activities. The strategy was still to give play to divisions within the top Indonesian elite by confining the Committee to a purely advisory role, and at the same time giving it the widest possible agenda. With no compulsion to arrive at detailed or specific decisions, and with an unprecedented opportunity to discuss all kinds of political problems, it was hoped that the secular nationalists and the Moslem leaders would become embroiled in endless debate and recrimination.[17] It says much for the leadership exercised by Soekarno and Hatta that when the B.P.K.I. eventually convened, these dangers were largely avoided, and the Indonesians skirted the trap laid for them by the military authorities.

On March 1, 1945, a Proclamation from the Gunseikan announced the formation of the B.P.K.I. to the Indonesian public.[18] The newly announced Committee was to study all matters that concerned the political and administrative framework of an independent Indonesian state. It was then to turn over its final report, its records and other documents to the Gunseikan, who would then send them for inspection and approval to the proper authorities in Tokyo. Eventually the approved materials would be sent back to a future Committee for the Preparation of Indonesian Independence, which would add the last touches and make the final formal decisions.

However once this announcement had been made, very little progress towards the actual inauguration of the B.P.K.I. seemed to take place in the following two months. Aside from the general considerations which led to the Japanese conception of the B.P.K.I. in the first place, two further considerations were probably important in accounting for the delay. On the one hand, the membership of the Committee was to be the product of joint discussions between leading Nationalists, the members of the *Dewan Sanyo* and the Japanese administration. Undoubtedly behind the

---

17 Nishijima, Kishi, *et al.*, *loc. cit.*, and p. 412. There was inevitably an air of contradiction about Japanese policy towards the political elite during this period. Co-operation was desired, but solely for war purposes. But elite cohesion was never anything but an apparently inevitable *means* to the mobilization of the population, not an end in itself. The obvious risks involved in promoting elite cohesion meant that the Japanese probably always had mixed feelings about following this policy. The basic opportunism of the policy accounts for much of the apparent confusion in Japanese activities during this period.
18 *Pandji Poestaka*, 23, # 5, (March 1, 1945), p. 131. *Soeara Asia*, March 1, 1945, p. 1. *Kan Po*, (March 10, 1945), pp. 26ff.

scenes a good deal of hard and protracted bargaining and manoeuvring took place. As we shall see, the eventual composition of the B.P.K.I. was scarcely representative of the three main Indonesian elites. Secondly, the Koiso Cabinet fell on April 5th as a result of the American landings on Okinawa on April 1st. Until the new Suzuki Cabinet settled itself into the saddle, it was inevitable that plans for Indonesia's future would be held in abeyance as far as possible.

At any rate, when a general meeting of the administrative heads of the various Southern Territories was held in Singapore late in March, the spokesmen for the 16th Army made it clear to their more cautious (and less harrassed) colleagues that they would go ahead with plans for the Committee regardless of what those colleagues might have in mind for their own territories — the discussions of the Committee would officially, and for the time being, be confined to the immediate future of Java alone.[19]

On April 29th, the Emperor's Birthday, was considered an auspicious occasion for two important developments. The cornerstone of a new State Training Institute (Kenkoku Gakuin) designed to produce an elite corps of highly trained young administrators was laid. More notable still, the membership of the B.P.K.I. was announced.[20] It was to consist

---

19 Present at this Conference were: General Dohihara, C-in-C, 7th Army Group (a prominent former member of the Kwangtung *Kodoha* clique); Lt. Gen. Ayabe, Chief of Staff, 7th Army Group; Major Gen-eral Isomura, head of the General Affairs Department, 7th Army Group; the heads of various other departments of the 7th Army Group's Headquarters; Major-Generals Umezu, Shimura, and Nishimura, representing the General Affairs Departments of the military administrations in Malaya, Sumatra and Java respectively. See *Statement* of Nishimura, April 25, 1947, p. 10.

20 Apart from Dr. Radjiman and R. Pandji Soeroso, the membership was:

Abikoesno Tjokrosoejoso	Hadji A. Sanoesi
Prof. Dr R. Asikin	R. Aris
B. P. H. Bintoro	Ki Hadjar Dewantoro
A.M. Dasaad	Drs. Mohammad Hatta
Ki Bagus H. Hadikusumo	Mr. Muhammad Yamin
R.A.A. Sumitro Kolopaking	Dr. R. Koesoemaatmadja
Mr. Alexander A. Maramis	K. H. Masjkoer
K. H. M. Mansoer	A. Kahar Moezakkir
Moenandar	Parada Harahap
R. Roeslan Wongsokusumo	Prof. Ir. R. Roosseno
Hadji A goes Salim	Dr. Samsi Sastrawidagda
Mr. R. Sastromoeljono	Mr. R. Pandji Singgih
Ir. Soekarno	R. Soedirman
Dr. Soekiman	Mr. A. Soebardjo
R. M. T. A. Soerio	Mr. Soesanto

of a Chairman, 2 Vice-Chairmen and 60 ordinary members, including 4 Chinese, 1 Arab and 1 Eurasian. There were also to be 7 Special Japanese members who would attend the Committee's sessions but would have no vote.[21] It was at first considered probable that Soekarno, as the pre-eminent nationalist leader, would take the chair, but apparently he was eager to take an active part in the debates, and after consultation with

K. H. A. Wachid Hasjim	Mr. Soewandi
K. H. Abdoel Halirn	Abdoel Kadir
Dr. R. Boentaran Martotmodjo	Prof. Dr. Hoesein Djajadiningrat
Mr. R. Hendromartono	Mr. Johannes Latuharhary
R. M. Margono Djojohadikusumo	R. Oto Iskandardinata
P. B. H. Poeroebojo	R. Abdoelrahim Pratalykrama
Mr. R. M. Sartono	Mr. R. Samsoedin
R. Soekardjo Wirjopranoto	Prof. Mr. Dr. Soepomo
Ir. Soerachman Tjokroadisoerjo	Drs. K. R. M. A. Soerodiningrat
M. Soetardjo Kartohadikoesoemo	R.A.A. Wiranatakoesoema
K. R. M. T. H. Woerjaningrat	Nj. M. Ulfah Santoso
Nj. Soenarjo Mangoenpoespito	K. R. M. T. Wongsonagoro
*A. R. Baswedan	*P. F. Dahler
*Liem Koen Hian	*Tan Eng Hoa
*Oei Tjong Hauw	*Oeij Tiang Tjoei

Those names marked with a star are non-ethnic Indonesians. See *Makloemat Gunseikan*, in *Kan Po*, # 66, (May 10, 1945), pp. 9f. Also *Soeara Moeslimin*, III, # 10, (May 15, 1945), pp. 8f. Cf. also A. G. Pringgodigdo, *Berdirinja Negara Republik Indonesia*, N. V. Pustaka Indonesia, Surabaja, 1958, p. 25.

On June 26th, 8 further appointments were made to the B.P.K.I. These were:

Mr. Mas Besar Martokoesoemo	Ir. P. Mohammad Noor
R. Asikin Natanegara	H. A. Fatah Hassan
Chaeroel Saleh	Soekarni
Abdoel Kahar	Bendoro K, P, Ario Soerjohamidjojo

Asia Raya, June 26, 1945. Cf. also Sutter op. cit., Appendix D, p. 1271f. However Chaeroel Saleh and Soekarni, designatecd as representatives of the youth, refused their appointments. Asa result they were dismissed from their jobs in the *Sendenbu* (Propaganda Department). This story is partially corroborated by the testimony of Yoshio Ichibangase, as reported in Prof. Dr. I. J. Brugmans et al., eds. *Nederlandsch-Indie onder Japanse Bezetting, Gegevens en documentan over de jaren 1942-1945*, Uitgave T. Wever, Franeker, 1960, p. 588. He agrees that the youth representatives refused their appointments, but says there were three of them and that the new appointments numbered 6.

21 Pringgodigdo, *op. cit.*, p. 25, says there were 8 such members. So does Yoshio Ichibangase himself, in Brugmans *et al.*, *op. cit.* p. 588. *Soeara Moeslimin Indonesia*, III, #10, (May 15, 1945), p. 8f., gives 7. It may be that *Soeara Moeslimin Indonesia* excluded Yoshio Ichibangase from its count since he was First Vice-Chairman. The Japanese members were:

Yoshio Ichibangase	Mitukiyo Matsuura	Masamitu Itagaki
Teichiro Ide	Minoru Tanaka	Tokuzi Tokonami
Toyohiko Masuda	Shozo Miyano	

Asia Raya, April 29,1945. Nishimura, in his *Statement* of May 31-June 6, 1946,p. 2, gives the same list, omitting only the name of Toyohiko Masuda. For an account of the role of the Japanese members, see Nishijima, Kishi *et al.*, *op. cit.*, p. 413

Hatta, he urged the appointment of the elderly, well-known nationalist Dr. Radjiman Wediodiningrat. The First Vice-Chairman was the Japanese Resident of Tjirebon, Yoshio Ichibangase, the second R. Pandji Soeroso, then Resident of Kedu.[22]

The composition of the B.P.K.I. is instructive in a number of ways. Broken down by age, one gets the following distribution:[23]

Where these two sources differ, I have followed the former.

Age	Number	Percentage
25-29	1	1.6%
30-34	1	1.6%
35-39	9	14.5%
40-44	11	17.7%
45-49	14	22.6%
50-54	11	17.7%
55-59	10	16.1%
60-64	4	6.5%
65-69	1	1.6%
	62	99.9%

The average age of the Committee is just over 48 years. In view both of the comparatively low life expectancy in Indonesia, and of the enormously important role the 'youth' were to play in the achievement of independence, it seems fair to conclude that the Committee is disproportionately weighted on the side of age. This is made even clearer when we remember that Hatta and Soekarno were at this time 44 and 45 years old respectively. Secondly, of the 11 members of the first three above

---

22 Soeroso was also designated head of the B.P.K.I.'s secretariat, assisted by Toyohiko Masuda and Abdul Gafar Pringgodigdo. See *Asia Raya*, June 5, 1945; *Kan Po*, #67, (May 25, 1945), p. 21. Pringgodigdo had earlier been secretary to the Visman Commission for Constitutional Reform which had convened to discuss the status of the East Indies in 1941. In fact, owing to the other duties for which Soeroso was responsible as Resident of Kedu, and to the negligence of Masuda, the bulk of the B.P.K.I.'s administrative work was carried on by Mr. Pringgodigdo and his two young lawyer-assistants, Mr. Assaat and Mr. Iskandar Gondowardojo, both later to become prominant in the nationalist movement.

23 See *Soeara Moeslimin Indonesia*, loc. cit., and Sutter, op. cit., p. 1271f.
Where these two sources differ, I have followed the former.

groups, 2 were women and 3 non-ethnic Indonesians. Thirdly, the only member of the group that could be called 'youthful' (25-29 years old) was a young aristocrat from Jogjakarta, sent to represent the Sultanate.

In 1944 the Gunseikan's office had produced a roster of prominent Indonesians living on Java, covering about 2000 names, The roster was drawn up under the direction of Dr. Hatta, and included brief career biographies of each member listed. According to the general classifications into which these 'prominent Indonesians' were divided the B.P.K.I., as it was composed in April 1945, can be broken down as follows:

General State Administration	4	6. 5%
Pamong pradja (civil service)	10	16. 1%
State Finance	0	—
Security	0	—
Justice	3	4. 8%
Business	7	11. 3%
Information (Propaganda)	3	4. 8%
Law	3	4. 8%
Health	4	6. 5%
Education	1	1. 6%
Culture	0	—
Religion	7	11. 3%
Politics	10	16. 1%
Youth	0	—
Not mentioned	10	16. 1%
	62	100. 0% [24]

In some ways this classification is rather misleading, in that, for example, the four 'health' officials were also active politicians, as were some of the members listed under 'law' and 'information'. Nevertheless the main groupings are made fairly clear. If we combine 'general state

---

24 See *Orang Indonesia Jang Terkemuka di Djawa*, Gunseikanbu, 1944, *passim*. Those members of the B.P.K.I. not mentioned in this roster were: the 4 Chinese, the Arab and the Eurasian, and, among the ethnic Indonesians, K. H. Masjkoer, P. B. H. Bintoro, Nj. Mr. Maria Ulfah Santoso and R. Abdoelrahrnan Pratalykrama.

administration', *'pamong pradja'* and 'justice', we shall have 17 members of the Committee (27. 4%) as civil servants dating from the pre-war period. This group approximately represents the *prijaji elite*. Combining 'health', 'law', 'education', 'information' and 'politics', we shall have the core of the secular nationalist elite represented on the Committee. This group numbers 21 (or nearly 34%). The Islamic elite is represented primarily by the 7 'religious' members (11. 3%). It is therefore readily apparent that Islam was heavily outweighed on the Committee, with the secular nationalists and the administrator *prijajis* each commanding nearly twice its strength. Educationally too, the Islamic elements were at a great disadvantage. Whereas almost all the members of the two other elites had had a fairly extensive Western-style education, and the administrators of course had accumulated a good deal of 'executive' experience, generally speaking the Islamic representatives had neither.[25] These factors, in addition to their numerical inferiority, were to have serious consequences for the Moslem group, not only in the manoeuvring within the B.P.K.I., but in the struggle for pre-eminence within the nationalist movement as a whole.

---

25 AbdoelHalim : No school education. Member of various Ulama groups before the war. First executive experience was being a member of the C.A.C.

Hadikusumo : Schooling in Koranic law in Mecca, Worked as a teacher and as a director of the pre-war modernist *Moehammad-ijah* 'welfare and education' organization. Member of the C.A.C.

Moezakkir : Religious education in Mecca and Cairo. A teacher all his life.

Sanoesi : Religious education in Java, and later Mecca. Writer of religious tracts. Sole political experience was being a member of the Bogor Provincial Council.

W. Hasjim : Local religious schooling. Associated with the pre-war traditionalist Nahdatul Ulama. Political experience confined to membership of the G. A. C. and the directorate of Masjumi's predecessor, the M. I. A. I.

K. M. Mansoer : Extended education in modernist Islamic schools in Mecca and Cairo. First executive experience: membership in the directorate of the Putera.

Dr. Soekiman : Western-style education, culminating in medical school in Amsterdam. Worked as a doctor and as an active politician in pre-war Islamic political organizations.

Three other members with Islamic connections were Hadji Agoes Salim, Abikoesno and Prof. Dr. Djajadiningrat, all of high educational standing, widely experienced, and, especially in the case of the first two, with strong affiliations with the secular nationalists. This group was to be important as a mediator between the secular nationalists and the Islamic leaders in the forthcoming debates of the B.P.K.I., though generally throwing their weight to the side of the former,

Two notable omissions in the B.P.K.I.'s memberships were the absence of any representation of the youth or of the pre-war 'leftist' political organizations. It was probably to correct the first omission or at least to acknowledge the growing influence of the youth, that, as previously mentioned, Chaerul Saleh and Soekarni were offered seats on the Committee in June. Nevertheless, even with two representatives, the youth would have been under-represented, both in proportion to the population and to their actual political influence. And as for the pre-war 'leftists', though Soekarno and Hatta are reported to have urged the Japanese to give a fair representation to the pre-war political parties, there was little that could be done in this case. Almost all such 'leftist' elements were underground or in jail.[26]

Between the announcement of the membership of the B.P.K.I. on April 29th and the opening of its first session on May 28th, one very significant development took place. On May 13th, Nishimura, head of the General Affairs Department, called the members of the B.P.K.I. together to brief them on developments at home and abroad, in the light of which they were to direct their deliberations. He revealed for the first time in public the news that Germany had capitulated, but declared that Japan had decided to carry on the war on her own. Even more significant was his statement that the military authorities would assume complete neutrality on "the religious question." As the General put it:[27]

> "Although we clearly recognize the ties between the Indonesian people and Islam, the Dai Nippon Government has absolutely no blue-print or plan on the status of the Islamic religion in the New State, or on its relationship to other religions, since, as I have already explained, it is for the Indonesian people to give substance to their own ideals in the formation of the New State; and Nippon will merely offer its help."

Taken in conjunction with the fact that Islam was represented by only

---

26 The *Partai Komunis Indonesia* was 'illegal' or underground. Sjahrir and his group were underground. Amir Sjarifuddin was in prison.
27 *Djawa Baroe*, III, # 10, (May 15, 1945), pp. 4f. gives the full text.

7, or at the outside by 10, members of the B.P.K.I., this statement was a serious blow to the general political position of the Masjumi, and more particularly to those elements in it who might have been expecting powerful Japanese support when the Committee came into session. The statement makes it probable that the small representation of Islam in the B.P.K.I. was the result of a deliberate decision of the Japanese. One can hardly doubt, in the light of the events of the First Session of the B.P.K.I., that the ease with which Soekarno dominated the proceedings and managed to impose his will on the Committee, was partially due to this shift in Japanese political strategy. Now that the Japanese had given a clear indication that they were no longer prepared to use the usually more 'co-operative' Islamic elite to balance off the secular nationalists, the prestige and self-confidence of the latter rose markedly.

The first session of the B.P.K.I. opened with a good deal of pomp and publicity on May 28th. The Committee was gathered together in the old C.A.C. building. General Itagaki, Commander of the 7th Army Group, and General Nagano, now Commander of the 16th Army attended personally. The Japanese and Indonesian flags were hoisted side by side above the Committee's conference rooms.[28] After General Nagano's formal inaugural speech, General Yamamoto, the Gunseikan (head of civilian administration) issued a series of instructions to the Committee. This in turn was followed by a formal speech of welcome on the Committee's behalf by the Chairman, Dr. Radjiman Wediodiningrat. The public was told little about the agenda or the debates of the Committee.[29] It was officially stated that this would allow the members of the Committee to discuss the important problems they faced in a more open manner.[30] The

---

28 For an account of the occasion, see *Soeara Asia*, May 28th, and G. Pakpahan, *1261 Hari Dibawah Sinar Matahari Terbit*, publisher unknown, no date (1948?), p. 122. Also by *Makloemat Saikosikikan # 2*, April 29th, the flying of the Indonesian flag, the *Sang Merah Putih*, was permitted on buildings designated by the Gunseikan. See *Kan Po*, # 66, (May 10, 1945), p. 9. The Japanese were also from now on forbidden to use the word Gen-zyuumin ('natives' or 'inlanders'), but rather the word *Indonesia Zin*; and *Indonesia-go* (the Indonesian language) was substituted for Marai-go (Malay).

29 See Brugmans *et al.*,eds, *op. cit.*, p. 588, for a statement by Ichi-bangase that the occasions on which the Committee would meet were kept a secret so as to prevent 'outside' influence on the Committee members. He adds that "several groups of students and other youths, with the support of certain committee members, asked to attend the meetings as interested bystanders. The chairman forbade this, which under the circumstances was very understandable."

30 *Kan Po*, # 66, (May 10, 1945), *Makloemat Gunseikan* # 23, p. 10.

press could add little more than that the Committee "had stayed up till 1 A.M. on the 30th discussing important problems."[31]

A final statement was eventually issued, declaring *inter alia* that the Committee deeply resented the landing of the Dutch on Morotai, Tarakan and Papua, and their attempts to invade Halmahera; rejected the Netherlands Indies Civil Affairs Administration and the idea of colonialism; was ready, along with 70 million other Indonesians to fight with all sincerity for Dai Nippon Teikoku; looked forward to the rapid realization of Indonesian Independence in order to carry out the final expulsion of the Dutch; and rejected the idea of a "mandate status", planned for Indonesia at the San Francisco Conference, as unfit for a free Indonesia.[32] In answer to these resolutions, the Japanese thanked the members of the B.P.K.I. for the sense of responsibility they had shown, and urged them to spend the time until the next session of the Committee in writing out their ideas and conceptions for an Indonesian Constitution to be instituted after Independence.

Generally speaking the three days of the first session of the B.P.K.I. were taken up with formal speech-making, and elaborate analyses of certain prominent members' 'state-philosophies.' By far the most notable of these was the future President Soekarno's outline of what was later, under the name of the *Pantjasila*, to become the official philosophy of the Indonesian state. The principles that make up the *Pantjasila* are well-known: nationalism, international humanism, popular sovereignty, social justice and the belief in God. These themes can almost all be found elsewhere in early post-war Asian socialism, and represent an attempt to synthesize modern European socialist ideas with more traditional indigenous conceptions. Yet the sources of Soekarno's thinking, and his very personal style of expression are so well brought out in this speech, that it may be appropriate to examine it in some detail.

In the course of his speech, the future President of Indonesia declared:[33]

---

31 *Soeara Asia*, June 2, 1945; *Asia Raya*, June 2, 1945.
32 *Soeara Asia*, June 1, 1945; *Kan Po*, # 68, (June 10, 1945), pp. 12f.
33 Prof. Mr. Hadji Muhammad Yamin, ed., *Naskah Persiapan Undang-Undang Dasar 1945*, Jajasan Prapantja, Djakarta, 1959, p. 73. There is no indication in Professor Yamin's edition as to the sources he has made use of, but it is probable that he has relied mainly on the official minutes taken down by Mr. A. G. Pringgodigdo, who was secretary to both the B.P.K.I. and the P.P.K.I.,

> "In 1918, thanks be to God, there was another man who recalled me (to my task), and that was Dr. Sun Yat-sen. In his work "San Min Chu I" or "Three People's Principles" I found a lesson which exposed cosmopolitanism. In my heart since then there has flourished a sense of nationalism through the influence of the Three People's Principles."

And indeed Soekarno's Nationalism, Popular Sovereignty and Social Justice clearly run parallel to Sun Yat-sen's Min Tsu, Min Chuan and Min Sheng, though certainly Soekarno's rhapsodic and eloquent expression of his Principles contrasts sharply with his mentor's dry and academic style.[34] In speaking of Internationalism Soekarno mentioned Gandhi's phrase, "I am a nationalist, but my nationalism is humanity." Yet perhaps Soekarno's internationalism is better seen as growing out of his experience with Marxist and socialist ideas than as a reflection of Ghandhian influence. His glowing references to Lenin in this same speech seem to support this suggestion. There is reason to believe that Soekarno's emphasis on the belief in God (*ketuhanan*), which of course finds no parallel in the writings of Sun Yat-sen and Lenin, stemmed both from his keen awareness of the place of religion in Indonesian life and from his experience as an exile in Flores between 1933 and 1938. There he had been in close contact with Roman Catholic priests and missionaries, and had reportedly become increasingly convinced of the 'equivalence' of different religious inspirations.[35] Certainly such a concept would also evoke deep resonances in traditional Javanese religious attitudes. In his speech Soekarno said:[36]

> "every Christian should believe in his own particular God. The

---

though of course as an active member on both bodies himself, Professor Yamin has presumably also drawn on his own personal recollections.

34 Cf. Dr. Sun Yat-sen, *San Min Chu I*, trans. Frank W. Price, China Committee, Institute of Pacific Relations, Shanghai, China, 1927, *passim*.

35 Soekarno himself however remained a Moslem, and even carried on a public debate through magazine articles on the subject of the problems of Islam. His opponent was the then youthful Mohammad Natsir.

36 Yamin, ed,. *op cit.*, pp. 77f.

Christian should worship God according to the teachings of Jesus Christ, Moslems according to the teachings of the prophet Mohammed, Buddhists should discharge their religious rites according to their own books. But let us all have belief in God. The Indonesian state shall be a state where every person can worship God in freedom... without religious egoism. And the state of Indonesia should be a state incorporating the belief in God! Let us observe, let us practise religion whether Islam or Christianity in a civilized way. What is the civilized way? It is the way of mutual respect." (clapping in the audience)

Yet at the same time Soekarno also repeatedly appealed directly to his Islamic colleagues on the Committee, doubtless through them addressing the whole powerful organization of Islam. Most significantly, in discussing the principle of popular sovereignty, he declared:[37]

"For Islam this is the best condition for the promotion of religion... the House of Representatives, this is the place for us to bring forward the demands of Islam. If we are really an Islamic people, let us work hard so that most of the seats in the People's representative body that we will create, are occupied by Islamic delegates... then the laws made by this representative body will naturally be Islamic laws too. We say that 90% of us follow the Islamic religion, but look around you in this gathering and see what percentage give their votes to Islam! To me it is a proof that Islam does not yet flourish among the masses."

The challenge could hardly be clearer. Considering the methods by which the Committee's membership had been chosen it was scarcely surprising that the percentage of ardent Moslems was not 90. The Committee however accepted the *Pantjasila*, and thus dealt another major blow to the Islamic cause and the Islamic State. The acceptance of *Pantjasila* by the

---

37 *Ibid.*, pp. 74f.

Committee further emphasized the ascendancy of the secular nationalist leaders over their rivals. If the Moslem groups had won the first round by avoiding incorporation into a monolithic nationalist movement, they had lost the second in the B.P.K.I.

Before breaking up on June 1st, the B.P.K.I. decided to set up a subcommittee under Soekarno to be responsible for analyzing and classifying suggestions for the future Constitution. All Indonesians were urged to send in any proposals or suggestions they might have to this committee. In the days that followed all the members of the B.P.K.I., particularly the Special Members,[38] were very active, going round from Residency to Residency conferring with administrative officials, holding meetings with youth groups and other organizations, and generally stirring up as much interest as possible in the fact of the Committee's deliberations.[39] On June 22nd, Soekarno organized a joint meeting of the B.P.K.I. Subcommittee, those members of the B.P.K.I. who also sat on the C.A.C., as well as any others that happened to be in Djakarta at the time. The meeting was held in the head offices of the *Djawa Hookookai*, and was attended by 38 people. This group then appointed its own subcommittee of 9 members to act as an executive and drafting committee. As a matter of fact, with the exception of Yamin, this new subcommittee was made up of the same men as those appointed to the B.P.K.I.'s subcommittee. They were:

Soekarno	Hatta	Maramis	Muzakkir	Abikusno[40]
Soebardjo	Yamin	Wachid Hasjim	Hadji Agoes Salim	

The main product of this Committee's work was a preamble for the new Constitution later to become famous, and controversial, as the Djakarta Charter. The main body of this Preamble was a catalogue of the crimes committed against the Indonesian people by the Dutch, and an eloquent

---

38 For the ostensible tasks of these members, see *Kan Po*, # 66 (May 10, 1945), p. 10. They were supposed to keep the Indonesians informed of Japanese law and customs as they might relate to the new Constitution and state structure. In effect they were appointed to keep a sharp eye on the Committee's discussions.
39 See *Asia Raya* for May and June 1945 for reports from various Residencies.
40 Prof. Mr, Drs. Notonagoro, *Pemboekaan Oendang-Oendang Dasar 1945*, Penerbitan mengenai Pantjasila, Nomor Kedua, Universitas Gadjah Mada, Jogjakarta, 1957, p, 13,

tribute to the glories of Indonesian power and civilization before the arrival of the Dutch East India Company. Suitable tributes to the inspiring example of Japan, as the leader of Asia's struggle against the imperialist West were also included. Lastly, a description of the history of Indonesia's struggle for independence was appended. The climax of the Preamble read as follows:[41]

> "And now the struggle of the Indonesian movement has reached a stage of happy and prosperous welfare, in which the Indonesian people have been led to the gateway of the Indonesian state, which is free, united, sovereign, just and prosperous, and which lives as a sincere member of the Greater East Asian Family...
>
> Thanks to the blessings of Almighty Allah, and basing itself on all the principles heretofore enumerated, and inspired by the glorious ideal of being master of its own fate and of a life for its people that will be free, honourable, respected, the Indonesian people hereby
>
> Declare their Independence!
>
> In the name of Allah, All-Loving and All-Merciful, in order to establish a Government for the Indonesian State; to protect the whole Indonesian people and territories; to promote the public welfare; to raise the standard of living; to develop our livelihood within the Greater East Asian family; and to participate in establishing a world order which is founded on freedom, eternal peace and social justice, National Independence is set forth in a Constitution of the Indonesian State, which forms a Republic based on people's sovereignty, *founded on: the belief in God, the obligation to carry out the commandments of Islam for all its adherents,* on the basis of a righteous and civilized humanity, the unity

---

[41] Notonagoro, *op. cit.*, pp. 35-38.

of Indonesia, and a democracy led by the wise guidance of the Representatives' Congress ensuring social justice for the whole Indonesian people."[42]

It should here be noted parenthetically that, as we have already mentioned, the Japanese had made almost no serious preparations for the sessions of the B.P.K.I., aside from their share in selecting its membership. No blueprints for the achievement of Independence had been drawn up. No final word had come from Tokyo. Most Japanese officers regarded the Committee essentially as a sop to Nationalist sentiment.[43] Although many of them, especially those in the 16th Army, were well aware of a rising popular restiveness, they were psychologically unprepared to do much more than play for time. Outside Java, many military men subscribed to the so-called "three-year plan" — which envisioned one year of preparation of the 'basis' of independence, one of preparation of independence itself, and one of the 'completion' of independence.[44] Without any firm ideas about what the Committee was or was not supposed to do, there was some difficulty in knowing just what to 'stop' at the Committee's discussions. It appears that the Japanese were caught unprepared by the boldness and insistence of the Indonesian leaders. The Indonesians on the other hand, regarding the Committee in a somewhat jaundiced light, were determined not to let themselves be played with by the Japanese. They intended to make the Committee a platform from which further demands could be made, far more concrete than hitherto.[45]

---

42 The italics are the author's. The phrase underlined was to be the subject of great controversy both at the second session of the B.P.K.I. and at the first meeting of its successor, the Committee for the Preparation of Indonesian Independence (which later became the *Komite Nasional Indonesia Pusat* or K.N.I.P.). The reader is therefore urged to bear it in mind.

43 Nishijima, Kishi, *et al.*, *op. cit.*, p. 411. On May 20th, a second Military Conference was held at Singapore, with almost the same people present as at the first. The only notable changes were that General Itagaki had replaced General Dohihara, and that for the first time the Navy (10th Area Fleet HQ in Singapore) sent representatives. The Java command reported on its preparations for the forthcoming meeting of the B.P.K.I. The Navy seems to have been rather uncooperative, insisting that its territory was 'special' with unique problems demanding 'unique' (i. e. Navy) treatment. Though the Conference was called primarily to co-ordinate the activities of the four commands on the nationalist and other questions, it does not seem to have accomplished much beyond an exchange of views and information. Cf. also the *Statement* of Nishimura of April 25, 1947, p. 12. Also *Statement* of Major-General Fumie Shimura, June 13, 1946, pp. 3f.

44 Nishijima, Kishi, *et al.*, *op. cit.*, p. 417.
45 *Ibid.*, p. 412.

With this more positive objective in mind, the Indonesians certainly held the upper hand through the remainder of the B.P.K.I.'s life.[46] When the second session opened on July 10th, and the Committee as a whole for the first time engaged itself in drawing up specific programs and a Constitution, Japanese ideas, such as they were, were firmly set aside.[47] The Army had expected Indonesia to emerge as a sort of semi-feudal monarchy, perhaps with the Sultan of Jogjakarta at its head. But here the Army underestimated the cultural differences between the Japanese and Indonesian traditions. They failed to realize that many of the Indonesian leaders had had far more extensive Western education than they themselves, and, apart from a small minority, were set upon creating a Republic, in its most non-monarchical sense.[48] From his own perspective, the Japanese Vice-Chairman of the B.P.K.I. summed up the reasons for the collapse of the Army's expectations. He listed four: i) the Islamic members supported a Republic because, according to Islam, political affairs should be decided by "common deliberation." ii) Many members believed that whatever state structure was instituted by the Committee would last only for the duration of the war. Thereafter, at a gathering of a National Congress, a permanent structure would be erected, iii) Though Indonesian nationalism inclined to monarchy, it was hard to decide which of the Javanese princes should fill the office. iv) If the Sultan of Jogjakarta should be selected, no one could be sure that the people from the Outer Islands or from the Sundanese areas on Java would accept him.[49]

With really remarkable speed, the B.P.K.I. at its second session drew up a Constitution and laid down the draft outlines of the future Indonesian state, covering such problems as: the extent of Indonesia's territory, citizenship, religion and political organizations. The problem of territory was essentially whether the new Indonesia would include British North Borneo, Brunei, Sarawak, Timor, Malaya and New Guinea. The Committee finally voted on the question as follows: 39 for all of the above, 19 for the former territory of the Dutch East Indies, 6 for the

---

46 Cf. the testimony of Ichibangase in Brugmans, *et al.*, eds., *op. cit.*, p. 588.
47 For example, the Japanese request that the Indonesians vote only on disconnected proposals. See Brugmans *et al.*, eds, *loc cit.*
48 Nishijirna, Kishi, *et al., op. cit.*, p. 414.
49 Brugmans, *et al.*, eds, *op. cit.*, p. 589.

former East Indies combined with Malaya, and omitting New Guinea, and 2 for other proposals. The Greater Indonesians thus won their point.[50] The question of citizenship was rooted in the difficult Chinese problem. The debate on their status divided not only the ethnic Indonesians but the Chinese representatives themselves, who were split between an 'assimilationist' and a 'non-assimilationist' group. The formula finally arrived at was that "citizens shall be native Indonesians and those of other races who are confirmed as citizens by law."[51] But this clearly meant that the assimilationist forces, as represented by Liem Koen Hian for the Chinese and P.F. Dahler for the Eurasians, had lost their battle for the automatic inclusion of their minority groups as Indonesian citizens. The formula effectively put off any final decision on this question till after independence.

The religious problem was perhaps the most delicate that the B.P.K.I. had to face. The Islamic members pressed for a full and strong recognition of their religion in the Constitution. This would have involved not only the power interests of the Islamic elite, but also assured the superior legal status of Islamic law (*hukum*) in the new state. However the demands of this group were strongly resisted by most of the other members of the Committee. Debate became particularly sharp over the important phrase of the draft Preamble, already quoted: "*the obligation to carry out the commandments of Islam for all its adherents.*" The Islamic group was very dissatisfied with the vagueness and ambiguity of this commitment. It was not clear whether the obligation was legally binding or merely 'moral,' a serious political principle or rhetorical phrase-mongering. It was equally unclear just who were "adherents," whether the phrase covered all nominal Moslems (perhaps 90% of the population) or only those who proclaimed their personal commitment to Islam. The dialogue between the Moslem group and their antagonists became highly acrimonious. It was only by dint of Soekarno's personal persuasion and diplomacy that the Islamic leaders were induced to accept the phrase.[52] As a sop to Islamic sentiment,

---

50 Yamin, ed., *op. cit.*, pp. 187-210, 214.
51 Yamin, ed., *op. cit.*, p. 267; also *ibid.*, pp. 242-250, 344-356.
52 Ki Bagus Hadikusumo commented that the phrase implied special duties for Moslems. There would be thus one law for the nationalists and one for the followers of Islam. This would only lead to resentment and anger in the country at large once it was known. Furthermore, there would certainly be Moslems in the national government; yet how were these Moslems to carry

it was agreed that by Constitutional provision, any future President of Indonesia would have to be a Moslem, This however was a purely nominal concession since the political facts of life in Indonesia would ensure that any future President would be some sort of Moslem, the nub of the question being what sort — "committed" or indifferent. And the 'Constitutional provision' was silent on this point.[53] There is no doubt that the Islamic group on the B.P.K.I. were upset over the Committee's decision, and a Japanese source comments that the formula, when made public, aroused considerable hostility both among the nationalist youth and Indonesians from the outer islands,[54] as a vague and unsatisfactory compromise.

The political structure of the future Indonesian republic, as proposed to the B.P.K.I., was apparently largely the work of Soekarno, Yamin, Soepomo and Soebardjo, three of whom were later to become prominent figures in the first post-independence Cabinet. The draft Constitution was designed to create a highly centralized and powerful state. Proposals for a federal structure of government were voted down overwhelmingly, The main feature of the government itself was to be an extremely authoritative and independent executive, not responsible to any legislature but rather to a huge People's Deliberative Assembly (M.P.R. or *Madjelis Permusjawaratan Rakjat*), meeting once every five years.[55] The President would be elected by this Assembly by majority vote, and was not restricted to one term of office.[56] There would also be a traditional type of legislature (*Dewan Perwakilan Rakjat* or People's Representative Council). But it would play a quite subordinate role, though sitting in a body within the M.P.R. when that Assembly convened. The legislature would have few claims on the

---

out the commandments of Islam if, as the nationalists proposed, the Government was to avoid all religious commitments. Soekarno replied that if the phrase were left out, it would look as if no recognition was being given to Islam in the Constitution. Clearly this would have embarrassed the secular nationalists. Hadikusumo was attempting to use this card to force the nationalists to concede Islam a greater role. Abikusno finally stepped forward to convince the opposition. He said that he of course as a Moslem "naturally. would ask for what Mr. Hadikusumo hopes for. But we have made a compromise. and, as the Chairman has said, we must give and take. For the sake of unity, let it never appear to the outside world that we have conflicted in our interpretation in this case."
Cf. Yamin, ed., *op. cit.*, pp. 282-284, 371-376.
53 Yamin, ed., *op. cit.*, pp. 391-393. See also pp. 386f. for Hadiku-sumo's strongly worded final statement.
54 Brugmans *et al.*, eds, *op. cit.*, pp. 589f,
55 See Chapter II of the Undang-Undang Dasar 1945, as quoted in Yamin, ed, *op. cit.*, p. 28
56 See Chapter III, Articles 6 and 7, as quoted *ibid*.

President, while he would have an absolute veto on any action it might take.[57] Moreover the President was to have wide emergency powers, whose assumption and duration he alone had the right to determine. Although any regulation issued by the President during an emergency could be revoked by the *Dewan Perwakilan Rakjat* (D.P.R.) at its next session, the President alone decided when such a session could be held. Suggestions that democracy might be served by making the Cabinet Ministers responsible to the D.P.R. were decisively rejected. The Cabinet would be selected by and answerable to the President alone.[58] A High Court was to supervise an independent judiciary without, however, having any powers of judicial review.

After a good deal of discussion it was also agreed not to include a bill of rights in the Constitution. It was felt that articles of this kind smacked of 'liberalism' and 'capitalistic individualism', and as such were contrary to the principles of gotong-rojong (mutual co-operation) and the organic unified state. Yet largely on the insistence of Hatta, certain particular rights, such as the freedoms of assembly, association and speech, would be "provided for by law." They would thus not be matters of individual right, but moral obligations assumed voluntarily by the state.[59]

Finally on the subject of political parties, there seems to have been some warm debate. Reportedly Soekarno took a position strongly opposed to any organizations which at that stage at least threatened the unified and organized power of the new nation.[60] Accordingly, no mention of parties was included in the final draft of the Constitution accepted by the Committee.

---

57 See Chapter VII, as quoted in Yamin, ed, *op. cit.*, pp, 30f,
58 See Chapter V, as quoted *ibid.*
59 See Article 28, as quoted in Yamin, ed., *op. cit.*, p. 32, and, for the debate on these matters, pp. 287-300, 314-315.
60 Cf. Nishijima, Kishi *et al., op. cit.*, p. 414. No mention of this problem is made in Yamin, ed., op. cit. See also Beknopt overzicht van de onafhankelijkheidsbeweging in Oost-Indie, a memo submitted to Rear-Admiral Patterson on September 26, 1945 by Rear-Admiral Maeda, p. 2, where Maeda says that the lessons derived from the frustrations of nationalism through factionalism in the colonial period, now provided a powerful incentive to the centralized co-ordination of all revolutionary forces.

CHAPTER THREE
CHANGING JAPANESE POLICIES, JUNE-JULY 1945

Throughout the summer of 1945 the Japanese military position deteriorated rapidly. Already in April, the new Suzuki Government had resigned itself to ultimate defeat probably late in the year, and was casting about desperately for means to alleviate the coming catastrophe. By July the Government had been forced by the progress of the Allied armies to make a final decision with regard to the eventual fate of Indonesia. On July 16th, the commanders of the various Southern Territories had already been warned informally that a final Supreme War Council meeting on the problem was imminent. They were also given a resume of the decisions the Council would probably take. The Vice-Minister for War and the Vice-Chairman of the Joint Chiefs of Staff instructed the local commanders that the greatest care would have to be taken to ensure that independence "would be handled in a way that would enable the Supreme War Council's political objectives to be realized." The provisional date for independence would probably be some time in September, but the actual date in any one area would depend largely on the initiative of the commander in that area, and the timing of the expected Allied attacks. There were also assurances that the remaining differences between the Army and the Navy would finally be resolved.[1] The Supreme War Council convened on July 17th, and their decisions followed the course outlined in the unofficial instructions of the 16th. The central concern of the Conference was how to secure a solid base for the 16th and 25th Armies' defence of Malaya and Indonesia against an anticipated Allied assault. Accordingly, the local commanders

---
1 Nishijima, Kishi *et al., op. cit.*, p. 419.

in the area were now requested to notify Tokyo of their own views as to the timing for independence in each of their areas, though, as previously mentioned, the Council had provisionally settled on September, at least for Java.²

In response to these instructions, which were approved by the Japanese Cabinet on July 21st, a third regional military conference was held in Singapore on July 27th, under the chairmanship of General Itagaki. The meeting was attended by representatives from the military administrations in Java, Sumatra, Malaya and the Naval Territories, as well as a group of staff officers sent down from Saigon.³ At this brief meeting it was finally decided not to include Malaya along with the former Dutch colonial territory in the new Indonesian nation, and to schedule independence definitely for early September. Draft plans for the actual transfer of authority were worked out, ready to be used when Tokyo gave the final signal.⁴ However the local commanders and their representatives, though expressing themselves as confident about handling the details of carrying out an 'independence program', said that they would prefer if possible for the formal legal beginnings to be made in Tokyo. (This request was shortly afterwards rejected by Tokyo, which ordered those on the spot to do everything in their power to make independence look like a spontaneous Indonesian creation not a product 'made in Japan'.)⁵ The regional conference also decided that the time had come to create a Committee for the Preparation of Indonesian Independence (*Panitia Persiapan Kemerdekaan Indonesia*—P.P.K.I.) to make final arrangements for the transfer of power from the Japanese to the Indonesian leadership. The announcement of this Committee's establishment would be made all over the Indies on August 7th. Its membership would be drawn from the entire Indonesian territory, proportionately to population. The Committee would then proceed to work under general instructions from Terauchi in Saigon and under the immediate supervision of Itagaki in Singapore. It would hold its first meeting on August 18th, and would

---

2 Cf. Nishijima, Kishi *et al.*, *op. cit.*, p. 419. Also Aziz, *op. cit.*, pp. 246ff., for further details.
3 For a list of those attending, see the *Statement* of Nishimura of May 31-June 6, 1946, p, 3.
4 Nishijima, Kishi *et al.*, *op. cit.*, p. 420. Also *Statement* of Nishi-mura of May 31-June 6, 1946, p. 3, and his Statement of April 10, 1947, p. 10.
5 Nishijimaj, Kishi *et al.*, *loc. cit.*

use the recommendations of the B.P.K.I. as the basis of its discussions.[6] But though independence was ostensibly to be applied to the whole of Indonesia as a unit, supplementary instructions made it clear that it was in fact to be granted provisionally only to "major areas." "Those areas not yet ready for assimilation" would be incorporated into the new nation at a later date.[7] By leaving the nature of "major areas" undefined, the Japanese of course retained the initiative and left themselves an 'out' in the case of unexpected eventualities. On August 2nd, a further set of instructions was issued from Marshal Terauchi's headquarters, confirming the plans laid down at the July 27th Conference, and assigning now a definite date, September 7th, for Independence. Certain subsidiary stipulations governing the relations between the Imperial Government and the new nation were also appended. The most important of these were:

a) the Imperial Government would "recognize" the Indonesian Government at once.
b) Indonesia would be required to declare war immediately on Britain, Holland and the United States.
c) For the time being, the commander of the 16th Army on Java would act as Japanese Ambassador, though there would also be a special Minister attached who would be a military officer on active duty.[8]
d) The Indonesian Government would temporarily have to maintain a number of Japanese military officers on its staff either with official appointments or in an advisory capacity.
e) There would be no 'extraterritoriality'. but Japanese property rights would be treated on the basis of the status quo.
f) For the immediate future, "the Imperial Government will exercise guidance over Indonesia's relations with third nations."[9]

---

6 *Statement* of Nishimura, April 10, 1947, p. 10.
7 Nishijima., Kishi *et al, op. cit.*, p. 429.
8 *Ibid.*, p. 420, On August 9th, an Ambassadorship was created. The Ambassador was to be responsible for diplomatic negotiations, and the protection of Japanese citizens and their commercial rights. The Military Commander was merely then to complement in the Ambassador's work in matters of internal and external security. They were supposed to work in the closest harmony.
9 Nishijima, Kishi *et al., loc, cit.* Clearly "independence" was going to be quite limited!

Agreement was reached among the Commanders of the various areas of Indonesia that the four guiding Advisors to the new government would be the Chiefs of Military Administration of Sumatra, Java and the Naval Territory, and Admiral Maeda.[10]

On the eve of the destruction of Hiroshima, the overall lines of Japanese policy towards Indonesia were thus reasonably clear. The Japanese authorities were well aware from reports they had been getting from Java and elsewhere that nationalist sentiment was rising fast, They generally believed that Japanese influence had been strong enough to make sure that this nationalism was deeply anti-Western. As a consequence two rough stages of development seem to have been envisioned. In the short run, in the event of an Allied invasion of the islands, this national feeling could be counted upon to bolster an effective Japanese defence of the area, And with luck, providing that the war continued at least until December, a fully-fledged Indonesian state would have been created before the war came to an end. The Allies would find an unpleasant surprise awaiting them on their arrival. A regime would have been created owing a deep material and psychological debt to the Japanese, and with no reason to expect anything but merciless hostility from the Allies, especially the Dutch. The essence of this strategy was timing. The Japanese had to have two or three months to consolidate the Indonesian administrative structure and political authority, so that the Allies could be effectively resisted when they landed. However these calculations were abruptly annulled by the annihilation of Hiroshima. From August 6th onwards, events began to move beyond Japanese control.[11]

Meanwhile in Indonesia too the situation was developing rapidly. On the official level a Committee similar to the B.P.K.I. was set up on Sumatra as of July 25th. It was headed by Mohammad Sjafe'i, previously chairman of the Sumatran Central Advisory Council.[12] But though it did succeed

---

10 Nishijima, Kishi et al., *op, cit.*, p. 429.

11 Cf. Anonymous Japanese Officer, *Beschouwingen over de algemene en financiele voorbereiding van der Indonesische Onafhankelijkheidsbewe-ging door de Japaners*, June 21-23, 1947, p. 4. Also E. Brunsveld van Hulten, *Rapport over de Japansche Invloede op de Merdekabeweging en de Gebeurtenissen in de Augustdagfen*, July 24, 1946, pp. 2f. It is possible also that some Japanese had an eye to the postwar world, where Japan would benefit by having a major Southeast Asian country favorably disposed towards it.

12 Cf. Kahin, op. cit., p. 121. Its membership included:
Appointed members:

in holding one meeting from June 21st to July 2nd, it was insignificant for all practical purposes. From June 18th to June 21st, the eighth and final meeting of the Central Advisory Council on Java was held. On this occasion the Council exhibited an increasingly independent attitude on its 'suggestions.' It urged that all existing organizations on Java be abolished and absorbed into a new unitary movement, in which — and this was a significant change — important posts would be assigned to youth leaders and officers of the Peta corps,[13] on the ground that "they are so well-known

Teukoe Tjoet Hasan	Teukoe Moehammad Ali
Tengkoe Hasbi	Tengkoe Othman
Radja Kalimsah Sinaga	Dr. R. Pirngadi
Hadji Abdoel Azis	H. Abdoel Malik Karim Amroellah
A. R. Soetan Mansjoer	Radja Saoel Loembantobing
Dr. Moehammad Djamil	Datoek Perpatih Baringek
Sjamsoeddin	Rangkaja Moehammad Djamil
Moehammad Jasin	Ir. Indera Tjahaja
Tjikmat	K. H, Tjik Wan
Ir, Ibrahim	Mr. Abdoel Abas
Soetan Rahim Pasaman	Abdoel Katab
Makalan	Tji Hoa Tjiong
Oen Lam Sing	

Elected:

Moehammad Sjafe'i (W. Sumatra)	Chatib Soeleiman (E. Sumatra)
Tengkoe Damrah (E. Sumatra)	Teukoe Moehammad Daoed
Toekoe Njak Arif (Atjeh)	Broeeh [Beureuh?] (Atjeh)
Aminoedin (Riau)	Dr. Ferdinand Loembantobing
Abdoel Manan (Djambi)	(Tapanuli)
Dr. A. K. Gani (Palembang)	Soetan Sori Pada Moelia (Tapanuli)
Radja Pagar Alam (Lampung)	Masarlif (Bangka-Billiton)
Abdoel Radjak (Palembang)	Abdoellah (Bengkoelen)

There was one other unnamed member. The Vice-Chairmen were Abdoel Abas and Teukoe Njak Arif. See *Djawa Baroe*, III, #15, (July 15, 1945), p. 6. See also *Statement* of Major-General Fumie Shimura, June 13, 1946, p. 3.

13 The Peta (Pembala Tanah Air — Defenders of the Fatherland) was a Japanese-trained volunteer corps of young Indonesians. Though the officers were Indonesians, Japanese N. C. O. s were usually attached to each unit as trainers, advisors, and spies. The higher ranks of the Peta were often filled with non-military politicians who also held political posts in the *Djawa Hookookai*. Below the battalion and company level however, the Indonesian recruits were given a thorough professional training. For an interesting account of the conflicts between the Japanese and Indonesians within the Peta, see S. M. Gandsubrata, *An Account of the Japanese Occupation of Banjumas Residency, Java, March 1942 to August 1945*, Data Paper #10, Southeast Asia Program, Department of Far Eastern Studies, Cornell University, 1953, p. 19. For an account of the Peta from the Japanese side see Brugmans, *et al.*, eds., *op. cit.*, p. 536. (*Statement* of Lieut. -General Yoshiro Nagano). Cf. also the interesting *Statement* of Captain *Kiso* Tsuchiya of the *Beppan (Nanseitai)*, Military Intelligence, l6th Army, April 3-8, 1947, pp. 2-4. He gives 33,000 men in the Peta (cf. Brugmans, *et al.*, eds., *loc. cit.*, for a figure of 35, 853, and Aziz, *op. cit.*, p. 230, for one of 37, 000), He reports that on Java there were usually two Japanese officers and five or six N. C. O. s attached to every

among the people."[14] The Council also asked for: a speedy expansion of the Peta and other para-military organizations in preparation for Allied landings; the rapid transfer of administrative posts to Indonesian hands; and the further recruitment of young Indonesians into departments of government, state enterprises, and provincial administrations, to train them for positions of leadership in the young Republic.[15] Without going into the reasons, which will be discussed later, it is still important to note the great stress laid at this meeting on the role of the youth and its "military" organizations in a Council dominated by elderly bureaucrats and nationalist revolutionaries of twenty years standing or more. It was a sign of a change in the focus of conflict in Indonesian politics that set in at about this time. The main struggle was increasingly to take place between youth groups (and other semi-legal organizations), and the Japanese, with the older leaders temporarily assuming a less prominent role.

The Japanese ignored most of these requests, except those concerned with the expansion of military and para-military bodies. They had made their plans and these did not for the time being envisage a free hand being given to undisciplined 'young rowdies' who might well turn popular hostility against the Japanese themselves, rather than the Allies, if they were not kept under firm control.

The Japanese military strategy for the defence of Java was, however, one in which an expanded indigenous 'army' was essential. They had discovered from earlier island campaigns the terrible cost of fighting the Allies with their superior fire-power and air support, on the beachheads. Their revised strategy was therefore to have a three-tiered

---

battalion of 500 men. There were 66 battalions on Java, requiring from 330 to 400 Japanese officers to look after them. The general headquarters for the organization was in Bandung. There were also four subordinate district headquarters, each staffed with Indonesian and Japanese officers under a Japanese colonel. The Bandung Headquarters made use of about 40 men including a few Javanese.

The *Beppan* (or *Nanseitai* after April 1945) seems to have been a military intelligence organization at first, but got involved later, perhaps in December 1944, in active defence preparations. It operated under Colonel Obana who was attached to the staff of the 16th Army. The *Beppan* seems to have had the main responsibility for training the Peta. However, according to Tsuchiya, the line of command to the Peta did not always run directly from the 16th Army headquarters through Bandung to the district headquarters. The policy-controlling bureau for the Peta in Djakarta, the Giyugun Shidobu, was often in direct communication with the district headquarters.

14 Statement of Mr. Sartono, *Djawa Baroe*,III, # 13, (July 1, 1945), p. 7.
15 *Djawa Baroe*, III, # 13, (July 1, 1945), p. 9.

coastal defence. The outer ring, nearest the coast, and including the major cities, was to consist largely of Indonesian auxiliary forces. These would bear the brunt of the Allies1 opening onslaught. Behind them would stand a secondary line of Japanese troops, strategically placed to control the units in front of them, and prevent any attempts to collaborate with the Allies. This secondary line would be concentrated on the perimeter of Java's *massif central*, with local headquarters at Bandung, Solo, Malang, Madiun, etc. To maintain this line, a steady movement of supplies, arms and currency was set under way in the summer of 1945 into these upland depots, out of the main areas where the Allies might attack. Finally, high up in the hills, there would be a group of Japanese and Indonesians specially trained in the techniques of sabotage and prolonged guerilla warfare. The general expectation was that fighting between the enemy and the Peta on the shoreline would fire the whole population behind the anti-Allied cause. The hard core of Japanese regular troops would defend the almost impregnable mountainous heart of Java. If and when the Allies finally crushed them, the guerillas would remain a running sore on the body of the victorious Dutch or Allied administration. This should ensure "no peace in Java" for some time to come.[16]

To complement this military strategy, the Japanese Army decided to try to set up a new all-inclusive national movement. According to a Government Announcement of July 2nd, this movement would be called the New People's Movement (*Gerakan Rakjat jang Baroe* — G.R.B.), and would be based on the principles of the *Pantja Dharma* and the (now moribund) New Life Movement.[17] Its membership was to be determined by four men: Soekarno, Hatta (secular nationalists), Wachid Hasjim

---

16 See Anonymous Japanese Officer, *Beschouwingen..*, op. cit. pp. 4-6. Cf. also Oemar Bachsan, Peta dan Peristiwa Rengasdengklok, N. V."Melati Bandung", Bandung, no date, *passim*. Figures for the Japanese Army on Java are uncertain, but cf. *Beschouwingen.*, p. 31, for an estimate of 70, 000, and 40, 000 on Sumatra. In Djakarta, according to the *Statement* of Captain Tsuchiya, April 3-8, 1947, p. 6, there were two Peta battalions, or in other words, approximately 1, 000 men.

17 See *Kan Po*, #70, (July 10, 1945), p. 19, for the inauguration of this movement. The *Pantja Dharma* was a set of Five Duties to the Japanese Empire accepted by the sixth session of the C.A.C. See *Kan Po*, # 55, (November 25, 1944), p. 17. Essentially the duties were to fight fervently for Dai Nippon Teikoku and to devote all energies to the upbuilding of the Greater East Asia Co-Prosperity Sphere. They were, incidentally, an adaptation for Indonesian use of a traditional set of Japanese political commandments.

(Moslem) and R.A.A. Wiranatakusuma (*Prijaji* administrator). The Gunseikan added that the youth would be expected to take part in the work of the movement, but, it was implied, would confine itself to village propaganda activities and para-military training.[18]

The four leaders then proceeded to select an 80-man Preparatory and Organizational Committee, which included 4 Chinese, 1 Eurasian, 1 Arab, and 8 Japanese, including, significantly enough, a member of the all-powerful General Affairs Department. The Peta was for the first time given official representation in a national body, in the persons of Kasman Singodimedjo and Abdul Kadir, then the top Peta officers in Djakarta.[19]

---

18 *Kan Po*, #70, (July 10, 1945), p. 19. Also Pakpahan, *op. cit.*, pp. 129f

19 The members of this Committee were:

Ir, Soekarno
R, A. A. Wiranatakoesoema
Mr. J. Latuharhary
Mr. R. M. Sartono
R. Abikusno Tjokrosujoso
B. P. A. Soerjodiningrat
R. Sukardjo Wirjopranoto
R. M. T. A. Soerjo
M. Sutardjo Kartohadikusumo
R. Abdulrahim Pratalykrama
R. Kasman Singodimedjo
Mr. R. M. Soemanang
Wachid Hasjim
Mr. Muhammad Yamin
K. R. M. T. Woerjaningrat
R. Pandji Soeroso
Hadji A. Sanoesi
Soeprapto
Dr. Radjiman Wediodiningrat
Soeradiredja
Mr R. Hindromartono
B.M. Diah
Asmara Hadi
R. M. Harsono Tjokroaminoto
Dr. Mas Moewardi
Adam Malik
Nj. Trimurty
Nj. Mr, Maria Ulfah Santo so
Oey Tiang Tjoei
P. F. Dahler
Mr. R. Ali Sastroamidjojo
Jozef Hasan
Wikana
R. Soewirjo
Nj. Emma Poeradiredja

Drs. Mohammad Hatta
K. H. Mas Mansoer
Mr. Alexander Maramis
R. Oto Iskandardinata
Moenandar
Ki Bagus Hadikusumo
K. H. Abdoel Halim
R. Pandji Singgih
Abdoel Kadir
K, H, Masjkoer
Soetardji
Aboe
Dr, Buntaran Martoatmodjo
Ki Hadjar Dewantoro
R. Roeslan Wongsokusumo
Mr. A. Soebardjo
Hadji Agoes Salim
Aroetoho
Dr. Mas Moerdjani
Ir. P. Mohammad Noor
Zainoel Arifin
Chaeroel Saleh
Soediro
Soepeno
Chalid Rasjidi
Soetomo
Nj. Soenarjo
Dr. Soekiman
Liem Koen Hian
A. Baswedan
J. Jahja
Soekarni
Soediro
Pandoe Kartawigoena
K. R. M. T. Wongsonegoro

A number of youth representatives were also included probably because the Japanese wanted to keep them out in the open where they could be watched. It is significant that many of them were to become very prominent in the early days of the Revolution, and almost all were strongly anti-Japanese in outlook.[20]

However, apparently to avoid future misunderstanding and trouble, the head of the General Affairs Department, General Nishimura, handed the four top leaders a nine-point statement elucidating the scope and role of the new organization. He warned the leaders against "continuing discord", and at the same time specifically reserved command over youth organizations for the official governmental apparatus. Though the youth leaders might be given representation on the Preparatory Committee, their organizations would continue to be controlled by older appointees of the Gunseikan, assisted by Japanese "experts."[21] On July 27th, the names of the 15 members of the G.R.B.'s executive council were announced. They included 5 secular nationalists of various types (Soekarno, Hatta, R. Sukardjo Wirjopranoto, R. Oto Iskandardinata, Dr. Moewardi), 3 Islamic representatives (Wachid Hasjim, Nj. Soenarjo Mangoenpoespito and Mr. Moehammad Roem, the latter acting for the *Hizboe'llah*), 1 delegate apiece for the *Seinendan* and *Keibodan*,[22] 1 for the Peta (Abdoel Kadir), 1 *prijaji* administrator (R.A.A. Wiranatakoesoema), as well as Dr. Abdoel Rachman Saleh and Soepeno (youth groups?) and Mr. Subardjo. Soekarno was elected Chairman, with Dr. Doeharto as his

---

Oei Tjong Hauw
Opposite the names above, ¢ means 'member of the C.A.C.', means 'member of the B.P.K.I. and @ means 'youth representative'. See *Asia Raya*, July 4, 1945, p. 1. Also *Indonesia Merdeka*, I, # 6,(July 10, 1945), p. 7, for the names of the Japanese members, and that of Wongsonegoro, omitted from the list in *Asia Raya*.

20 For more information on the youth representatives, see Chapter IV, below, especially in their relation to the G.R.B.
21 *Indonesia Merdeka*, I, # 6, (July 10, 1945), pp. 6ff. See also Benda, *op. cit.*, pp. 192f.
22 The *Seinendan* was a youth corps for ethnic Indonesians between the ages of 14 and 25, who were trained in elementary military training, fire prevention, and air-raid defence. They were also given extensive physical education and instruction in the Japanese language. The corps9 most promising members were given heavy Japanese militarist indoctrination, and were often promoted into the Peta officers' class. The *Keibodan* was a similar 'boy scout' youth association, perhaps numbering as many as 1, 280, 000 young men. Cf. Aziz, op. cit., pp. 224-230; Benda, *op. cit.*, p. 252, n. 34; and *Japanese Report about Indo-auxiliary troops*, R. V. O., 006501-006506, 006527 as cited in Aziz, *ibid.*, p. 230.

secretary.[23]

Pakpahan claims that many meetings of the new Executive Council were held without the knowledge or participation of the Japanese.[24] Aziz however adds that lack of harmony among the leadership, their attempts to insert "republican" phraseology into governmental regulations, and their open discussion of "forms of government" so annoyed the Japanese that the movement "had to disappear."[25] Whether this was in fact the case or not, the G.R.B. was unlikely to amount to much as long as the *Djawa Hookookai* and the Masjumi, its largest components were not effectively integrated. And to the end of the occupation the Moslem organization managed to retain its own separate identity.

One other indication of the general tendency of the Japanese in this period to lean to the side of the "older" leaders, was the continuing trend towards the transfer of high governmental posts to Indonesians in this group. R.A.A. Wiranatakoesoema was appointed head of the Local Administration Division, Dr. Boentaran Martoatmodjo of the Health Division, Ki Hadjar Dewantoro of the Educational Division (all within the Interior Affairs Department) and Ir. Soerachman Tjokroadisoerjo of the Economic Affairs Department.[26] As we have already noted, Dr. Samsi was now *Sanyo* to the Finance Department, and Dr. Soepomo held the same position within the Justice Department. These appointments were symptomatic of the steady rise of Indonesians within the bureaucracy, and were part of an emerging pattern of dual authority, created in preparation for the transfer of power.

---

23 Cf. *Soeara Moeslimin Indonesia*, III, # 15, (August 1, 1945), p. 2.
24 Pakpahan, *op. cit.*, p. 136.
25 Aziz, *op. cit.*, p. 244; cf. also Benda, *op. cit.*, p. 193. See below, Chapter IV.
26 For these appointments, see *Kan Po*, # 71, (July 25, 1945) pp. 19f.

CHAPTER FOUR
YOUTH GROUPS, ILLEGAL GROUPS AND THE MASSES, TO THE SURRENDER

There can be little doubt that the Japanese Occupation was a 'traumatic' experience to a great many Indonesians. The initial reaction to the Japanese invasion had been in many quarters enthusiastic. The Japanese had been welcomed as delivering Indonesia from Dutch colonialism. But the sudden and complete collapse of Dutch power had more significant long-term results, leaving aside the special characteristics of Japanese military rule. The seclusion of the top echelons of the Dutch administrative apparatus in internment camps meant that a large number of Javanese who had previously held subordinate administrative posts had suddenly to be promoted. But at the same time, the actual prestige of such administrative positions was sharply reduced, both as a result of a deliberate early Japanese policy of humiliating the *pamong pradja* class,[1] and as an inevitable consequence of their identification in the popular mind with the previous regime. The new positions may therefore have been regarded by those who held them in a somewhat ambiguous light. Forced to assume unprecedented responsibilities, yet without real authority or great prestige, the *pamong pradja* as a group suffered a severe decline in morale, though doubtless their practical experience and competence was widened by the new duties they had to undertake.[2] Their standing within the Indonesian community can scarcely have been

---

1 See Gandasubrata, *op. cit.*, *passim.*, for the perspective of a member of this class on Japanese administrative policy, and on the changing position of (in his case) the Regent in wartime Indonesia.
2 Cf. some comments by three Indonesians on this question, as cited in Brugrnans, etal, *op. cit.*, pp. 159-161.

raised by their direct responsibility for two of the most hated aspects of the Japanese economic system: the forced deliveries of rice, and the recruitment of Romusha labour. The occupation thus seems to have been marked by a steady breaking up of traditional social relationships and hierarchies, at least partly as the result of deliberate Japanese policy. New elites, also encouraged by the Japanese, assumed an importance unparalleled in Dutch times. And there was every indication that the greater the autonomy Indonesia gained, the stronger the position of the more specifically *political* elements (particularly the Moslem and secular nationalist leaders) would become. There is good reason then to suspect that the more conservative members of the *pamong pradja* were at least ambivalent about the whole concept of Independence and the future it promised.[3]

The Islamic and secular nationalist elites of course experienced the effects of the occupation rather differently. The arrival of the Japanese enhanced their social and political prestige, and mass organizations like the *Djawa Hookookai* and the Masjumi enabled them to build a kind of popular underpinning for themselves which they had never been able to do during the later Dutch period. For the first time many of them were given opportunities to exercise 'responsible' administrative functions, although 'oppositional' residues, acquired through years of Dutch repression, in some cases persisted. Those who had a more extensive Western-style education tended, with some notable exceptions, to be psychologically un-attracted by if not contemptuous of the methods and personnel of the Military administration. Others rapidly turned strongly anti-Japanese, but were more lastingly affected by Japanese attitudes and working-styles.

But perhaps it was at the lowest level of Javanese society[4] that the occupation had its most revolutionary effects. A vast disruption of village life, already unsettled during the later Dutch period, was set in

---

3   Cf, the obviously bitter comments of "Javanicus" in Brugmans, ed., *op. cit.*, pp, 159f., who speaks of "upstart" young men from the *Keibodan* and other youth organizations intimidating local officials. He also notes the breakdown of the old distinctions between "*dorpers*" and "*prijaji*" (roughly "villagers" and "aristocrats") caused by Japanese centralization and militarization of the bureaucracy, as well as promotion policies by which inexperienced Japanese "favorites" secured positions traditionally reserved for the *prijaji*.
4   Javanese, of course, in the geographical not the ethnic sense.

motion. The autarchic policies of the Japanese Army, and the growing disruption of trans-Java communications, had disastrous consequences, Smuggling became widespread, both within Java, and beyond to Sumatra and Singapore, often as an indispensable condition of staying alive.[5] The ineffectiveness of Japanese countermeasures, and in some areas their open connivance, did nothing to diminish popular dislike for the 'barbarian' invaders. The drafting of the Romushas imposed a serious drain on the village economy.[6] The decline or diversion of textile production led to severe clothing shortages. Forced deliveries of rice had the same effect on food supplies in many areas. Inflation, fostered by irresponsible Japanese financial policies, pressed hard on the urban communities. A greatly accelerated rate of movement into the larger cities from the countryside was stimulated by Japanese educational training programs, youth organizations, propaganda and the declining prospects and attractions of village life. Nor were the cities in any condition to absorb this great migration. Traditional social structures and attitudes of deference were shaken by the Japanese treatment of established local notables, and the unprecedented attention paid to the youth.[7]

There is reason to believe that rural unrest in many areas had its origins in the last two decades of Dutch rule which helped to create a sizeable dispossessed and marginal 'rural proletariat.' The ferocity of the Japanese and the speed of the changes they introduced unleased long-suppressed dissatisfaction, hatred and other anomic and revolutionary impulses. On the positive side, the elaborate systems built up by the Japanese to mobilize popular energies and enthusiasm for the war effort through nationalist symbols did much to canalize the general unrest and give it a definite objective. Admiral Maeda himself compared the situation in Java in 1944-45 with that in Banten just prior to the Communist revolt in 1926-27, adding that the revolutionary forces were now a thousand times greater

---

5 Cf. above, footnote 25,
6 For the Romushas, see above, footnote 23. The removal of the Romushas often involved a transformation of the family division of labour, with the women assuming new roles.
7 For example, these notables were often made to do gymnastics, dig in the fields, wear unaccustomed and often undignified clothing, etc. Cf. also Brugmans,et al *op. cit.*, pp. 527f., for the observations of a Javanese Regent, on the recruitment of young schoolteachers and police officers into the higher ranks of Peta. Apparently a battalion commander in the Peta was accorded equal rank to a Regent (in the Dutch period, the highest rank in the Indonesian side of the civil service).

and a thousand times more conscious of themselves and their aims.⁸ The opportunities afforded to such leaders as Soekarno and Hatta, on the orders of the Gunseikan, to arouse nationalist sentiment by radio addresses and personal tours through Java and in the outer islands, were effectively seized to give 'specific' ideological channels to these revolutionary forces. Moreover, the *Djawa Hookookai*, which Soekarno headed, was able to reach down to the village level, where it was organizationally linked to the *Tonarigumi* (or Neighbourhood Associations).⁹ It was thus able to create an organized framework for the expression of strongly aroused nationalist (and anti-Japanese) aspirations.¹⁰ By 1945, for the first time in Indonesian history, there were political organizations continuously and fairly effectively connecting the rural family to the centres of political power and decision-making in the capital.

However popular unrest only began to take on a definitely political coloration on a broad scale in 1945. A number of outbursts and uprisings had previously taken place against the Japanese, but they had been mostly simple protests against the local exactions of particular military administrators, or other Army officers. But by early 1945 a much wider poli-ticization of the masses began to make itself felt, especially in the 'twilight zone' between the cities and the remote rural hinterland. The extent and depth of this revolutionary transformation seems to have been seriously underestimated by the major groups contending for power in Djakarta, Japanese, 'older' leaders, youth leaders and 'resistance' groups alike. Yet in the last analysis, it was the politicized masses that created the Revolution, and brought about its final triumph against the calculations of the returning Dutch, and of the outside world. Therefore, although much space will be devoted from here on to a discussion of youth and 'resistance' activities, the groundswell of revolutionary excitation among the masses in 1945 should always be kept in mind.¹¹

---

8 See *Beknopt overzicht van de onafhankelijkheidsbeweging in Oost-Indie*, memorandum of Admiral Maeda to Rear-Admiral Patterson, September 26, 1945, p. 3.
9 The *Tonarigumi* was a system of village organization imitated from traditional Tokugawa practice. It was designed to work as a two-way communications system between the government and the villages, passing orders and propaganda down, and intelligence information up the administrative system. Cf. Aziz, *op. cit.*, pp. 222-224. For an amusing Indonesian comment, see the observations of a 17-year old girl cited in Brugmans, *et al, op, cit.*, p. 162.
10 Cf. Aziz, *loc. cit.*
11 The two most important uprisings prior to Blitar had occurred in Tasikmalaja (March 1944) and

It is convenient to mark the opening of the new revolutionary period of the Occupation by the revolt of the Peta garrison in Blitar (Kediri) in February 1945. On the night of February 14-15th, Peta groups in Blitar carried out a surprise attack on the munitions depot, and seized key points within the city such as the headquarters of the Military Police and the telephone exchange.[12] A sizeable number of Japanese military men and local Chinese were massacred. According to the official report, not published until two months later, the mutiny was led by a young officer named Suprijadi, who had "mystical beliefs," and was resentful at not having been promoted with his fellow-officers.[13] An Indonesian source claims that though in fact Suprijadi was an ascetic and an "occultist," it was not this, or any question of promotion, but the procuring of local girls for Japanese officers by Chinese white-slavers, that had impelled him to revolt. But the source adds significantly that "the spirit implanted by the Japanese began to flare up in his heart and created resistance against his teachers."[14] The revolt itself was speedily crushed. Suprijadi himself disappeared, and was probably secretly executed by the Japanese. All the other leaders of the revolt were court-martialled. A number of high Indonesian civilian officials and Peta officers were summoned to witness the trials. Among these were Oto Iskandardinata, Kasman Singodimedjo, Mas Sudiro, Abikusno, A.K. Muzakkir and Dr. Supomo. The presence of Abikusno and Muzakkir, two prominent Islamic leaders seems to indicate that the Japanese wished to involve all the three major elites in a general condemnation of such anti-Japanese actions and to show that the punishment meted out was not an act of Japanese vindictiveness, but was approved by Indonesia's most trusted leadters. When the future President Soekarno was directed to speak on the affair, he skilfully avoided either condemning or condoning the mutineers directly. He simply said that "possibly it will have a damaging effect on the interests of Indonesia." But

---

Indramaju (September 1944). Cf. also an interesting report contained in Brugmans,*et al.*, *op. cit.*, p. 599; the author, an Indonesian, reporting to the Japanese authorities, notes the sudden rise early in 1945, of omens and signs of impending calamity, observed by *kampung* seers and clairvoyants."Generally the people are awaiting critical developments."

12 Aziz, *op. cit.*, p. 228.
13 Cf. *Kan Po*, # 67, (May 25, 1945), pp. 10-14; *Asia Raya*, May 19, 1945, p. 1; Pakpahan, *op. cit.*, pp. 108f.
14 Pakpahan, *op. cit.*, p. 109.

he hoped the generosity of the Japanese would induce the Government to mitigate the sentences of those convicted.[15] The local *prijaji* officials were disgraced and forced to resign, and after an investigation carried on for some weeks of the 68 accused, 8 were sentenced to death,[16] 12 were released and the rest received intermediary punishments.[17]

The Blitar revolt was certainly the most serious single attack on Japanese authority during the Occupation. It must have been deeply disturbing to the authorities, especially in view of the favoured treatment that they had accorded to the Peta. It is therefore rather remarkable how leniently (by Japanese standards) the offenders were dealt with. It is reasonable to assume (and the lack of publicity given the affair seems to confirm this) that the Japanese sensed that in the changing psychological atmosphere oft Java, severe repressions might only generate further resistance. Certainly it is unlikely that the authorities would have acted with such mildness a year before. Furthermore, as one Peta officer records it, Ms organization, which militarily speaking was an elite corps, gradually came to see itself as the vanguard of revolutionary nationalism. After early difficulties between commissioned and non-commissioned officers (caused partly by the Japanese policy of filling the former group with political appointees), began to subside, the local units of the Peta developed an increasingly intense esprit de corps.[18] The various para-military youth organizations, such as the *Seinendan*, *Keibodan* and *Heiho*, although less highly trained, were infected with the same spirit of messianic revolutionary ardour.[19] Special corps such as the *Barisan Pelopor*,[20] the *Hizboe'llah*, and the Kamikaze-like *Barisan Berani Mati*, were given special treatment and training on the best Japanese Patriot Army model. As has been suggested before, the main body of these organizations was made up of young

---

15 *Ibid.*, p. 110.
16 Two of these later had their sentences commuted.
17 Pakpahan, *loc. cit.*
18 Cf. Oemar Bachsan, *op. cit.*, passim, but especially sections 3 and 7.
19 In these latter units, the Japanese "style" seems to have been more influential. See Brugmans, *etal*, *op. cit.*, pp. 482f., for an interesting comparison between the Japanese military ethics of *Bushido* and some aspects of Javanese tradition.
20 See footnote 26, above. Cf. also Brugmans, *etal.*, *op. cit.*, pp. 544ff for some observations on the *Hizboe'llah*, which may have had as many as 50, 000 members by the end of the occupation; and Aziz, *op. cit.*, p, 230. It is hard to believe the *Statement* of Captain Kiso Tsuchiya, p. 3, that the numbers went as high as 500, 000.

men and adolscents of little formal education, who were enormously stimulated (often against the Japanese) by Japanese propaganda, and in whom the patterns to be expected of the Japanese military personality found an inevitable reflection. Xenophobia, radicalism, strong comradely loyalty, authoritarianism, superb, if almost suicidal courage, and a belief in salvation through direct action characterized all these units to a greater or lesser extent.[21] The revolutionary elan was not however confined to military and para-military formations. Under the influence of the general popular unrest, and the sedulous proselytizing of the "older" leaders as well as the para-military elements, the same elan was rapidly communicated to the student populations of the larger cities such as Djakarta, Surabaja, Bandung, Semarang and Jogjakarta.

There were also, particularly in Djakarta a number of "resistance" or "underground" organizations operating clandestinely against the Japanese. These organizations can be divided loosely into four main groups, though there were people in each "underground" who acted as 'overlap' or liaison members with the others. First there were the remnants of Amir Sjarifuddin's organization, which had largely disintegrated when the Japanese arrested Amir early in 1943.[22] These were people mainly from the more radical wing of the pre-war *Gerindo*, and from the "illegal P. K. I."[23] The second group, probably the most extensive by the summer of 1945, was headed by Sutan Sjahrir. His organization, with the most highly educated membership of the four, had branches in Tjirebon, Garut, Semarang and Surabaja; in Tjirebon Dr. Sudarsono succeeded in setting up an elaborate organization under the cover of a Japanese-sanctioned peasant co-operative system. The organization's activities seem to have been concentrated on intelligence-gathering and surreptitious anti-Japanese propagandizing. In close association with the Sjahrir group, and perhaps in some sense its 'junior partner' was the *Persatuan Mahasiswa* (Student Union) in Djakarta, consisting chiefly of students at the medical faculty there. Its members were generally younger, less 'underground' and, towards the end, more openly anti-Japanese in their attitudes and behaviour. Both the Sjarifuddin and the Sjahrir groups were opposed to

---

21 Maeda, *Beknopt Overzicht.*, pp. 2f.
22 For the story of Amir's arrest, see Pakpahan, *op. cit.*, pp. 97-99. Cf. also Kahin, *op. cit.*, pp. 111f.
23 For this section I am almost wholly indebted to Kahin, *op. cit.*, pp. 111-120.

the Japanese regime on ideological (anti-fascist) as well as on nationalist grounds. The other two 'underground' organizations were perhaps less ideological in their attitudes. One of these was the so-called Menteng 31 group, led by Chaerul Saleh, Sukarni, Adam Malik, Panduwiguna and Maruto Nitimihardjo. A number of these leaders had been employed in the *Sendenbu* (Department of Propaganda) and though they "resigned" their posts in June 1945,[24] they remained somewhat apart from the Sjahrir-*Persatuan Mahasiswa* group. Many of them had been given ideological training at the *Sendenbu*-sponsored *Asrama Angkatan Baru Indonesia*, located at Menteng 31.[25] As a result perhaps they were more attuned to the psychology of the Peta officers and other paramilitary groups, than to that of the Sjahrir group, though many of them supposedly remained under Sjahrir's influence.[26] Their main organization was in Djakarta though reportedly they had close associations with certain radical *kiais* in Banten.[27] The Japanese Military had certainly seen that their greatest chance of stirring up strongly Japanized anti-Western sentiment lay in capturing the allegiance of the younger student groups who had been least under Western (Dutch) influence, and could be expected to give an ideological lead to their non-university contemporaries.[28]

That this general classification of 'resistance' groups is reasonably accurate is partly borne out by the subsequent careers of the three 'groups'. The faithful in Sjahrir's group formed the nucleus of the post-independence *Partai Sosialis Indonesia*, with its strongly Western orientation and disinclination for organized state violence. Parts of the Sjarifuddin group eventually formed an important component of the

---

24 In fact they were removed by the Japanese. See *Statement* of Lieutenant-Colonel Hisayoshi Adachi et al., no date, p. 6. We shall see why below.
25 Cf, Kahin, *op. cit.*, p. 113, Bachsan, *op. cit.*, section 7. (He mentions that Soekarno, Hatta, Yamin and Iwa Kusumasumantri were invited to lecture there) See also for more details, Fakta dan Doku-men2 untuk menjusun buku "*Indonesia Memasuki Gelanggang Inter-nasional*", Subperiode: Kabinet Presiden Soekarno dari tenggal 17. 8. 45 sampai 14. 11. 45 (from Periode III-Dari Proklamasi Kemerdekaan ke Pengakuan Kedaulatan, dari 17 Agustus 1945 sampai achir Desember 1950) Kementerian Penerangan, Direktorat V, Seksi Penjelidikan dan Dokumentasi/ Perpustakaan, Djakarta, June 1958, pp. 150-153. This source notes that one of the most effective ways of spreading anti-Japanese propaganda was by means of a travelling theatre company, giving inflammatory performances in the *kampungs*.
26 Reportedly Sukarni, Maruto, Adam Malik and Panduwiguna were former pupils of his.
27 Cf. *Fakta dan Dokumen2..*, p. 152.
28 *Ibid.*, p. 150, describes the assortment of *betjak* drivers, laborers, schoolboys, drifters and students associated with this group.

resurrected Communist Party. And many members of the Menteng organization became associated with the radical nationalism of the *Partai Murba* and its first leader Tan Malakka.

The fourth group centred around the *Asrama Indonesia Merdeka* (Independent Indonesia Training-school) set up by Admiral Maeda, but effectively administered by his aides Shigetada Nishijima and Tomegoro Yoshizumi, with Mr. Subardjo and Wikana as their chief Indonesian colleagues. Other associates included Dr. Samsi, Dr. Buntaran Martoatmodjo, Mr. Latuharhary, Dr. Katulangie, Iwa Kusumasumantri and Tadjoeddin Noer.[29] The activities of this 'school' have been fully discussed elsewhere.[30] It is perhaps enough to say here that from October 1944 to July 1945 a small group of young men aged from eighteen to twenty, specially selected by Nishijima on the advice of his Indonesian intimates, were given extensive instruction in a wide variety of subjects, but with particular emphasis on so-called 'communism.' In fact this 'communism' seems to have been very closely related to the ideology of an important group within the Japanese Navy as a whole.[31] The dominant themes of the training given in the Navy's *Asrama* were anti-capitalism, anti-imperialism (Western) and a strong elitism.[32]

Kahin has discussed the various interpretations that have been put upon this "*Kaigun*" (Naval) school. These fall into two main categories: 1) The school was used by the Japanese to train 'infiltrators' who could penetrate the Communist and near Communist undergrounds and either control them (and eventually perhaps direct them against the Allies) or split them along pre-war lines (perhaps between the 'orthodox' group and the unorthodox 'nationalist-communist' Tan Malakka group). The main objection to this interpretation is that it leaves unexplained the strong Army hostility to this organization, supposing the group to be a genuinely anti-Communist infiltrating group, and the popularity of the organization's sponsors in Indonesia in the post-revolutionary years.

---

29 Kahin, *op. cit.*, pp. 115-120. However Dr. Ratulangie spent most of his time in Makassar.
30 *Ibid., loc. cit.* Probably not more than 25 or 30 people attended the school. Among them were Djojopranoto, Sudiro, and Chairuddin.
31 See above, Chapter I.
32 Among those invited to lecture at the school, on the initiative of Mr. Subardjo, were such figures as Soekarno, Hatta, Sjahrir, Iwa Kusumasumantri, Sanusi Pane, Dr. Buntaran, Mr. Maramis, Mr. Latuharhary and Sudiro (not the student Sudiro).

Moreover Wikana, who was a key man in the organization, seems to have been a *bona fide* Communist at this time,[33] and was keeping the various undergrounds closely informed of what was going on at the *Kaigun* office. 2) The school represented a genuine effort to create an echelon of Indonesian nationalist leaders who would serve two quite distinct purposes: a) in the case of an Allied landing and the death or capture of the older leaders Soekarno and Hatta, they would form a reserve group ready to take over and carry on the struggle. b) there seems to have been an anticipation among the 'Naval group' that in the event of an Allied victory, Japan would "go Communist" or at any rate sharply leftist; that the Allies would soon fall out, with the Anglo-Saxon powers arrayed against the Soviet Union; and that in such circumstances Japan might find herself in alliance with Russia. If this should prove the case, an Indonesian elite with radical anti-Western sympathies might prove useful in countering the influence of the Anglo-Saxon powers in Southeast Asia, and extending that of their adversaries. If this interpretation is correct (and it should again be emphasized that in this context "Communism" should not be taken to mean subservience to Russian interests), it accounts for the employment of Wikana as organizer for the *Asrama Indonesia Merdeka*, the hostility of the Army, and the exemption of Maeda and his group from Indonesian bitterness towards the Japanese, To this writer at any rate, it seems difficult to deny that there was a strong element of sincere and intelligent interest in Indonesian independence on the part of the *Kaigun* organizers.[34]

With this rough outline of the main organized groups involved, and the general "climate of opinion" on Java, we may be in a better position to follow the course of events of the summer of 1945.

From May 16th to 18th a meeting of the *Angkatan Muda* was held in the Villa Isola near Bandung. The *Angkatan Muda* (Young Generation) was a Japanese device, established in mid-1944, for controlling undesirable

---

[33] Before the war he had been a member of the radical oppositionist *Gerindo* party. It is uncertain when or to what extent he became a Communist.

[34] Cf. Kahin, *op. cit.*, pp. 115-120, and *Beschouwinger.*, p. 27f. with caution. This theory incidentally helps to account for the attraction of many of the *Asrama*'s pupils to Tan Malakka's organization. There are strong similarities between Tan Malakka's nationalism, anti-capitalism, anti-imperialism (Western) and "pan-Asian" internationalism, and what I have suggested was the ideological outlook of the *Kaigun* group.

elements among the youth. Those young men who were known or suspected of having "illegal" connections or who were persistently and openly hostile to the Japanese and at the same time influential among their comrades, were forced to assume leadership in the organization. The Japanese were thus able both to keep an eye on them, and implicate them in 'pro-Japanese' activities. In the middle and lower echelons of this organization of course they had their own agents and spies.[35] The Congress of the *Angkatan Muda* was attended by college and high-school students from all over java.[36] One Indonesian commentator reports that the Congress had been preceded by a demand in the Djakarta press[37] that the *Angkatan Muda* be "brought out of the wings" and allowed to push itself forward into all fields, both political and social "since it was the youth who would be the future builders and defenders of free Indonesia."[38] After the Congress, reports issued by the Japanese-controlled *Domei* radio network from Djakarta declared that the Congress had decided that only two alternatives could possibly be accepted by the youth of Indonesia — Freedom or Death. In this spirit the Congress had passed two resolutions: 1) That all Indonesian groups be united and centralized under a single national leadership. 2) Indonesian Independence should be realized as soon as possible — the *Angkatan Muda* was constantly prepared and ready to devote its physical and spiritual energies towards the co-ordination of all efforts in that direction.[39]

The two resolutions are significant. The first clearly attacks the divisions between the top secular nationalist and Masjumi leaders as weakening the unity of the drive for independence. Although "a single united leadership" was a phrase open to varying interpretations, it certainly postulated *prima facie* an all-inclusive leadership which the Masjumi elements could scarcely provide. In combination with Nishimura's statement of May

---

35 Kahin, *op. cit.*, p. 114. Among the more notable of the *Angkatan Muda's* leaders were Sukarni, Chaerul Saleh and Ruslan Abdulgani.
36 According to monitored Japanese broadcasts, there were 300 delegates from all parts of Java, and the purpose of the Congress was to prepare for the creation of a single all-Java youth organization, see *Federal Broadcasting Intelligence Service Daily Reports*, May 26, 1945, Section Q 2.
37 Since the press was tightly controlled by the Japanese, this "demand" must have had official approval or at least permission.
38 Pakpahan, *op. cit.*, pp. 118ff. For further details, see Soeara Moeslimin Indonesia, III, #12, (June 15, 1945), pp. 17f.
39 Pakpahan, *loc. cit.*

15th, mentioned earlier, by which the Army tacitly abandoned its efforts to balance the conflicting Indonesian elites, the youth resolution must have struck an ominous note in Islamic ears. If the *Angkatan Muda* was at all representative of the youth, the Islamic leaders faced still another contending group besides the older leaders, the *prijaji* administrative class, and the Army itself.

The second resolution revealed a barely concealed impatience with the slow pace of preparations for independence (probably the youth had the B.P.K.I. particularly in mind), and the older leadership for not pressing the authorities firmly and vigorously enough.

The Villa Isola Congress was followed by a series of youth conferences and meetings all over Java, particularly in the larger cities. There is perhaps therefore some reason to believe that the Congress was a turning point in youth activities in the pre-revolutionary period, somewhat similar to the inauguration of the B.P.K.I. for the older leaders, Like the B.P.K.I., the Congress allowed representatives from all parts of the island, speaking for all kinds of groups, to co-ordinate plans and proposals, compare ideas, increase their solidarity, and return to their own localities with a renewed self-confidence and a determination to spread their influence still further and deeper.

From June 18th to 21st, the eighth session of the Central Advisory Council was held. As suggested previously,[40] the most notable aspect of its discussions was the great emphasis placed for the first time on the role of the youth, and the pleas made to the Japanese government to bring more young people into the administration, expand their military training, and include them in the leadership of the projected G.R.B. (*Gerakan Rakjat jang Baru*). The motivation of the older leaders at this C.A.C. meeting remains open to conflicting interpretation. One observer comments that "the mounting revolutionary fervor of the recently formed youth organization, *Angkatan Muda*, had exerted strong pressures on the not entirely unwilling, if not even (sic) intimidated, councillors. The call for the inclusion of youth and military leaders in the national leadership, may, therefore, in part at least have been the genuine expression of a widely shared, growing Indonesian impatience, primarily caused by

---

40 See above, pp. 37-38.

Japanese dilatoriness in transferring authority. The resolution may, in such an interpretation, have had the backing of the established, older leadership, constituting a direct challenge to the Japanese authorities. On the other hand... the *Angkatan Muda*'s claim to a prominent place in the nation's councils may not only have been intended as a challenge to continued Japanese authority but, at the same time, as an equally emphatic challenge to the divided ranks of the older leaders... The Council's advice would then, in that case, have been brought about by moves of which the established Indonesian leadership, in particular Soekarno and Hatta, had no knowledge, and which they had, therefore, not approved."[41]

The second interpretation seems the more difficult to maintain, in its entirety at least. At the beginning of the session, the Vice-Chairman, Kusumo Utojo, had been replaced by Hatta on the grounds of *age*. Soekarno was already Chairman.[42] The demands for the inclusion of youth representatives were forwarded most notably by Mr. Sartono, one of Soekarno's most loyal followers. Moreover, a curious episode recorded by an Indonesian writer throws an illuminating sidelight on the events of C.A.C.'s meetings. According to this account, a mass meeting was held in the Taman Raden Saleh in Djakarta by students of the Medical College, the Law Faculty, the Japanese-sponsored State Training Institute and the secondary schools of Djakarta. On the urging of a student at the State Training Institute, three resolutions were adopted: 1) The youth should prepare themselves to carry on the struggle however bloody.[43] 2) The youth of Indonesia should stand firmly on the principle of the total unity of all sectors of society. 3) In order to be able to defend their country the youth must be prepared to undergo intensive military training. A representative from the Medical College declared that:

> "Everywhere throughout the world, it is the youth who are always revolting to combat inappropriate modes of acting and thinking. The youth must now agree to undergo training in military barracks."

---

41 Benda, *op. cit.*, pp. 191f.
42 Pakpahan, *op. cit.*, p. 126.
43 Note that there is no mention of whom the struggle is to be against.

Armed with a further unspecified resolution, the crowd marched off to Soekarno's house. The future President tried to calm them:

> "I will work as hard as I know how to have your resolution put into effect... I see that my younger friends out there are carrying a banner reading 'Freedom for the People!' That is completely in harmony with our Pantja Dharma."[44]

When the youth groups reached Hatta's house, the same demands were pressed. The future Vice-President answered briefly:

> "I am delighted to see all you young people here. Unity among the youth like this is something I have long dreamed of. *Be sure that you will all of you soon replace the present leaders, who are getting old.*[45] I myself will work hard to see that all your aspirations are fulfilled."

The commentator adds "it was as though they were still uneasy about the urgings of the youth; so that they only answered 'they would work hard so as to get things done.'"[46] If this report is accurate, the almost apologetic note struck by the two leaders leads one to surmise that they had a very shrewd idea of what the attitudes of the youth were, but were faced with an awkward dilemma. It was all very well to make use of the youth groups' impatience as a means of pressuring the Japanese into accelerating the attainment of Independence. But it was clearly a very difficult thing to try to turn these youth demonstrations "on and off," as the occasion warranted. Such open and premature agitation must have had its alarming as well as its encouraging aspect. There was always the danger that the youth would bypass their leadership and come into open conflict with the Japanese authorities. The resolution of the C.A.C. can therefore perhaps be best interpreted as an adroit attempt to kill two birds with one stone:

---

44 This comment is a little curious since barely two weeks before Soekarno had specifically rejected the *Pantja Dharma* in favour of the *Pantja Sila* (at the first meeting of the B.P.K.I.). For a note on the *Pantja Dharma*, see footnote 91, above.
45 The writer's italics.
46 Pakpahan, *op. cit.*, p. 125.

stimulate the Japanese to hasten independence, and satisfy the clamour of the militant youth groups, — and possibly tap the energies of some of the youth leaders in semi-administrative jobs, or military exercises.

If we accept the idea that the older leadership was already somewhat anxious about youth activities, their anxiety can only have been increased by another extraordinary incident that occurred in Surabaja at about the same time. At a Japanese-sponsored meeting of about 4, 000 students, the official opening speech stressing that Indonesian independence could be obtained only by Indonesians fighting alongside the Japanese against the Allies, was roughly interrupted by a member of the *Angkatan Muda*, who said he agreed with the necessity of fighting for independence, but denied that it would be against the Allies. The meeting's speeches were being broadcast all over Java, and the thunderous applause which greeted this challenge must have been heard in many parts of the island. The Japanese had no recourse but to break up the meeting by turning on the air-raid sirens.[47]

The main concentration of the *Angkatan Muda* apparently centred around Bandung. However, according to Tan Malakka, a second youth organization, "with its own conceptions," called the *Angkatan Baru Indonesia*, was set up in Djakarta on June 15th, 1945.[48] Though there was a good deal of overlapping between its leadership and that of the *Angkatan Muda*, it seems to have been more radically minded, possibly because its leaders were drawn largely from the Menteng 31 group.[49] It was nearer the centres of power in Djakarta, and, though like the *Angkatan Muda* it was sponsored by the Japanese, it seems to have been smaller and less thoroughly infiltrated by the regime. Its leading figures were, according to Tan Malakka, Chaerul Saleh, Harsono Tjokroaminoto, Sukarni, B.M. Diah, Supeno and Wikana.[50] It was within this group that the plans

---

47 Recounted in Kahin, *op. cit.*, p. 122.
48 Tan Malakka, *Dari Pendjara ke Pendjara*, "Widjaja," Djakarta, 1948 (?), Volume III, p. 53.
49 For comments on the two youth organizations from the Japanese side, see the *Statement* of Lieutenant-Colonel Hisayoshi Adachi, *el at.*, p. 8.
50 Tan Malakka, *loc. cit*, Cf. also Darmosugondo, "Mengenang per-istiwa sekitar 17 Agustus 1945", in Darius Marpaung, ed., *Bingkisan Nasional*, P. T."Usaha Pegawai Nasional Indonesia," (P. T, "Upeni"), Djakarta, 1956 (?), pp. 42f., for further details on the *Angkatan Barn Indonesia*. He gives the executive committee as being composed of: B.M. Diah (*Asia Raya*), Sudiro (HQ *Barisan Pelopor*), Sjarif Thajeb, Harsono Tjokroaminoto (*Madjalah Masjumi*), Wikana (*Kaigun*), Chaerul Saleh (*Sendenbu-Barisan Pelopor*), F. Gbeltom (*Seinendan*), Supono, and Asmara Hadi (Liaison

for a *coup d'etat* against the Japanese which were to become, if only psychologically, an important factor in the events of the Proclamation of Independence were laid.[51]

It is worthwhile in this connection to follow Tan Malakka's movements in these last months, and his relationship to these youth organizations, though doubtless his account should be accepted only with caution. According to his own story, he was working at this time as assistant to the head of the Rangkas (Banten) branch of the *Badan Pembantu Keluarga Peta*,[52] and that his chief was one of the delegates to the May 16th congress of the *Angkatan Muda*. On returning from the Congress, he told Tan Malakka of incipient plans discussed by the delegates for merging all youth organizations on Java. After the establishment of the Angkatan Baru Indonesia in Djakarta, the sentiment for this merger became even stronger, and a conference was supposed to assemble in Djakarta late in June to discuss the details. Tan Malakka was thereupon asked by his chief to go to represent the Rangkas district at this conference. But he arrived in Djakarta only to find that the conference had been cancelled on the orders of the Japanese Army, Though he tried to make contact with Wikana and Panduwiguna "whose names I had heard previously", he succeeded in reaching only Harsono Tjokroaminoto, Anwar Tjokroaminoto and Chaerul Saleh, without however revealing who he was. Disappointed by the cancellation of the conference, he was compelled to return to Banten.[53]

Tan Malakka also claims (and to some degree his interpretation is corroborated by Nishijima) that the *Gerakan Rakjat jang Baru*,[54] or at any rate the important role assigned to the youth in that movement, was a deliberate tactic on the part of the Japanese to mollify youth sentiment for the cancellation of the proposed Djakarta conference.[55] If this is correct, it suggests how alarmed the Japanese were becoming at the activities of the younger generation. The situation was particularly delicate for them,

---

between *Barisan Pelopor* and the *Djawa Hookookai*).
51 See below, Chapter VI.
52 An organization to provide financial and other aid to the families of Peta men on active duty away from home.
53 Tan Malakka, *op. cit.*, p. 53.
54 For other aspects of this organization and its establishment, see above, Chapter III, pp, 39-41.
55 Tan Malakka, *loc, cit,* Cf. Nishijima, Kishi, *et al.*, *op. cit.*, p. 485.

since their plans for a general mobilization of the population for the Allied invasion did not allow them to give these prominent youth leaders the short shrift which would have been easy a year earlier. Moreover as Kahin points out, many of the youth leaders were sons of important nationalist politicians and other widely respected figures.[56]

Further insight into the difficulties the Japanese were confronted with is provided by the story of the session of the G.R.B.'s Working Committee and particularly its debate on the creation of a united youth organization for all of Java. At the opening meeting on July 6, controversy apparently arose immediately on the use of the word "Republic" in the charter the G.R.B. was drawing up for itself. The Subcommittee headed by Soekarno, Hatta, Subardjo, Yamin and Abikusno prudently advised simply putting the word in brackets, as indicating a future state of affairs. According to Tan Malakka, the "main body" of the conference was extremely dissatisfied with this advice.[57] A climax was reached when the senior Japanese officer present handed Chairman Soekarno a note and asked him to read it aloud to the audience. The contents of the note simply said that the "Republic" question was one which the Emperor alone had the right to decide, A great hubbub ensued, in which one source states that "Soekarno lost control of the meeting."[58] Chaerul Saleh spoke harshly against the cautious tactics of the older leaders and told them that if they persisted, their efforts would be sabotaged by the youth. He warned the Japanese that the Indonesian people was no longer willing to await orders from Tokyo.[59] Finally, possibly by pre-arrangement,[60] Adam Malik stood up and shouted that he and his friends had come to the conference "to speak for the people" and that if the people's will was going to be frustrated, he saw no reason to stay. With that he stalked out, followed by Chaerul Saleh, Sukarni, Chalid Rasjidi, Wikana, Trimurty, B.M. Diah, Supeno, Sudiro (mBah), Sutomo, Panduwiguna, Harsono Tjokroaminoto, Asmara Hadi and Muwardi.[61]

---

56 Kahin, *op. cit.*, p. 114, n. 20.
57 This sounds rather unlikely, considering the make-up of the body, which except for the youth leaders, seems to have been 'older generation' and rather cautious in its approach.
58 Tan Malakka, *op. cit.*, p. 54.
59 *Fakta dan Dokumen2*, p. 153,
60 According to *Fakta dan Dokumen2*, *loc. cit.*, the youth had held a strategy meeting just before the big G.R.B. session.
61 Inferred from *Fakta dan Dokumen2*, *loc. cit.* Tan Malakka, *loc. cit.*, says only Chaerul Saleh, Sukarni, Panduwiguna, Diah, Trimurty, Wikana, Sudiro (mBah), Chalid Rasjidi and Supeno

Whether in fact this incident is true in all its details (it is obviously directed against Soekarno and Hatta), it is certainly 'in character' for the period. A 'dare-devil' psychology[62] was being generated among the youth by their growing sense that the defeat of the Japanese was impending. Though the Japanese Military Police (*Kempeitai*) remained active and vigilant, its psychological ascendancy was diminishing rapidly.[63]

On August 4, a statement was issued in the name of Soekarno and Hatta, the two top leaders of the G.R.B., summoning an All-Java Youth Congress to meet some time in the middle of the month. But this statement had to be withdrawn suddenly, on the grounds that the two leaders "had to devote their energies to more important matters."[64] It is possible that this was the case, but it is perhaps more likely that the Japanese had once again cancelled such plans.[65] Various important youth leaders prominent in the *Angkatan Muda* were ordered to go out and pacify their followers by stressing the genuineness of these "more important matters" and the fact that the Congress was really only being postponed, not cancelled. Clearly there was a strong suspicion among the rank and file that neither was true.

With the beginning of August, the schools were breaking up for the holidays. Partly, one suspects, to get the students out of the big cities where they might cause real trouble, loose all day, the Japanese authorities began by ordering all those enrolled in the State Training Institute to scatter over the countryside to the remotest village "in order to get experience

---

walked out. The others remained. Incidentally *Fakta dan Dokumen2, loc. cit.*, makes Chaerul Saleh the leader of the walk-out. Cf. also Brugmans, *et al, op. cit.*, pp. 566f., statement of Hideo Ohashi of the *Sendenbu*, who says that Soekarno ordered a temporary adjournment, which was later made permanent.

62 Stimulated no doubt by competition and rivalry among the youth groups as to who could 'outdare' the others.

63 Lieutenant-Colonel Adachi *et al.*, in their *Statement* say that the Military Police effectively broke up the *Angkatan Baru Indonesia* late in July. See p. 8. Considering the looseness of these organizations, and their semi-official character, it is hard to know what this meant in real terms. The psychological position of the *Kempeitai* as the Revolution approached has an interesting histori-cal parallel in the situation of the AVOs on the eve of the Hungarian uprising in October 1956.

64 Pakpahan, *op. cit.* pp. 136, 138.

65 They can hardly have been reassured by Soekarno and Hatta's wording of the initial announcement, which, as Pakpahan notes, contained none of the usual effusive expressions of gratitude and loyalty to Dai Nippon. For this whole incident, see Pakpahan, *op. cit.*, pp. 136-139.

and enlarge their outlook."[66] As Nishimura, head of the General Affairs Department, gently put it, "throughout that summer we had growing difficulties in keeping them in line."[67]

---

66 Pakpahan, *op. cit.*, p. 137.
67 *Statement* of Nishimura, April 10, 1947, p. 3.

CHAPTER FIVE
SAIGON

Early in August a reluctant Marshal Terauchi received final instructions from Tokyo as to the course independence should take.¹ The order was signed by both the Japanese Government and the Supreme War Council. Accordingly on August 7th, he proclaimed throughout the areas under his command that permission had finally been granted for a "Committee to Prepare Independence for Indonesia" (*Panitia Persiapan Kemerdekaan Indonesia* — P.P.K.I.). The Committee was to be set up immediately:²

> "In acknowledgement of the efforts and sincerity of the inhabitants of Indonesia, the Commander-in-Chief of the Southern Territories expresses his approval for the institution, towards the middle of August 1945, of a Committee for the Preparation of Independence. This Committee is to speed up the final measures to be taken to establish a government for an independent Indonesia."

A supplementary announcement however by the Gunseikan, General Yama-moto, added that:³

> "The first condition for attaining independence must be winning the war... Indonesia will also have to develop her

---

1 W. H. Elsbree, *Japan's Role in Southeast Asian Nationalist Movements, 1940-1945*, Harvard University Press, Cambridge, Massachusetts, 1953, p. 94. Cf. also Aziz, *op. cit.*, p. 251, quoting statement of Numata Takazo, Chief of Staff to Marshal Terauchi, that these orders had come to his superior from General Anami himself, the Minister of War.
2 *Asia Raya*, August 7, 1945.
3 *Kan Po*, # 72, (August 10, 1945), p. 12.

resources so that in co-operation with Dai Nippon a final victory in the war may be achieved for Greater East Asia... This Preparatory Committee is to be formed in Java, and its purpose is to complete the last preparations for independence for the whole of Indonesia, so that when all the preparations in Java are completed, this will mean that all the areas of Indonesia will become free in a new state."

At the same time the old B.P.K.I. was quietly and informally disbanded. Yamamoto thanked it for its services, and reminded its members that the members of the new Committee would be selected this time not just by the 16th Army, but by Marshal Terauchi himself on the advice of the regional commanders.[4] The representatives for Java were then chosen by Yamamoto and Nagano, the Commander of the 16th Army, and their names were passed on first to Itagaki in Singapore, and then to Terauchi.[5]

On the same day that the Terauchi proclamation was made, a group of top military officers met at Itagaki's orders in Djakarta to do the "real work" that the P.P.K.I. was ostensibly supposed to do before independence could be obtained. Those present at this meeting were General Nagano, Commander of the 16th Army, General Shimura of the 7th Army Group, Admiral Maeda, General Hamada of the Sumatran command, General Nishimura, Captain Yanagihara of the Kaigun, and Major Mori, liaison officer between Singapore and Djakarta, in addition to a large staff.[6] On Tokyo's insistence, and in spite of their apparent conviction that the task was impossible, the Committee worked "night and day" to solve the difficult problems of transferring power, financing the new regime,[7] and deciding on the concrete role to be played within that regime by Japanese civilian and military personnel. As reported by Colonel Jano, political

---

4 *Asia Raya, loc. cit.*
5 *Statement* of Nishimura, May 31-June 6, 1946, p. 3.
6 *Statement* of Nishimura, May 31-June 6, 1946, p. 4. Cf. also Y. Ita-gaki, "Outline of Japanese Policy in Indonesia and Malaya during the war with special reference to (the) Nationalism of (the) respective countries," *Annals of the Hitotsubashi Academy*, Vol. II, # 2, April 1952, p. 186.
7 It was decided that the Indonesians should use Japanese Army currency till they could produce a currency of their own, and the early financing of the regime would be carried out by the Southern Areas Development Bank. See *Statement* of Nishimura, May 31-June 6, 1946, p. 4.

advisor to Marshal Terauchi, he had received on July 29th a secret wire from Tokyo saying that "in principle the Emperor grants independence to the Indonesians, nevertheless this should only be proclaimed if Russia's participation in the war becomes inevitable." On August 5th word again came from Tokyo, this time warning the Marshal that "within a few hours Russia will declare war on Japan, and therefore the Marshal should summon Soekarno and Hatta to tell them of the Japanese Government's decision to grant independence."[8]

Accordingly on August 8th, Soekarno, Hatta and Dr. Radjiman Wediodiningrat left Djakarta by plane for Singapore and Saigon. Accompanying them were Dr. Soeharto, Dr. Radjiman's physician, General Shimura, Lieutenant-Colonel Nomura, head of the Planning Section in the General Affairs Department of the 16th Army, and Miyoshi, a civilian aide and interpreter on General Nishimura's staff.[9] What exactly happened at the meeting of the Indonesian leaders with the Marshal is a little obscure. Kahin reports that on August 11th, Terauchi promised the three leaders that Indonesia would be made independent on the 24th, after a Constitutional Assembly had been convened on the 19th to add finishing touches to the constitutional draft already drawn up by the B.P.K.I.[10] General Shimura gives early September as the date assigned for the transfer of power,[11] Nishijima asserts that Terauchi told the three Indonesians that no fixed date would be set, though the P.P.K.I. would be inaugurated on the 18th. Furthermore, the final territory to be included in the new nation would cover only the former Netherlands Indies. Independence would start in Java, and thence would be extended stage by stage through the outer islands. Japan would also reserve certain rights and privileges for the duration of the war, and would expect the P.P.K.I. to

---

8 Transportation had become so precarious between Tokyo and South East Asia that already in late July it had been decided that the official Indonesian 'visit' to receive the symbols of Independence would be made not to Tokyo, as had for example been the case with the Burmese, but to Marshal Terauchi, as the highest accessible representative of the Imperial Government. Cf. *Statement* of Nishimura, May 31-June 6, 1946, p. 5. Jano's remarks were made in an interview with Nathan Brock of the *Christian Science Monitor* on August 30, 1946. (Cited in Wirjodiatmodjo, *op. cit.*, pp. 38f.)

9 *Statement* of Nishimura, April 25, 1947, p. 7. *Statement* of Shimura, June 13, 1946, p. 4. Brugmans, *et al*, *op. cit.*, p. 594, gives Miyoshi's report.

10 Kahin, *op. cit.*, p. 127. Interestingly enough, this implies that the Japanese must have accepted the B.P.K.I. 's constitutional draft with very little change.

11 *Statement* of General Shimura, June 13, 1946, p. 5.

maintain close contact with, and accept the guidance of, a Guidance and Communications Bureau (*Dokuritsu Jumbi Shido Renraku*) of Japanese officers, which would be established separately in Djakarta.[12] Hatta relates that at an official meeting on the 12th, Terauchi told him that "we leave it up to you to decide when Indonesia is to become independent."[13] Soekarno later declared at the opening session of the P.P.K.I. that he had told the Marshal that in spite of the B.P.K.I.'s claim to Malaya, New Guinea, British North Borneo, Portuguese Timor, etc., he would be content with the territory of the former Netherlands Indies.[14] In view of the decision taken at the Itagaki Committee's previous sessions,[15] it seems that Nishijima's is probably the fullest and most exact of these accounts. In any case, it can be safely said that after the atom-bombing of Hiroshima on the 6th and Nagasaki on the 9th, Tokyo was no longer con-cerned to obstruct the formation of an independent Indonesia — she no longer had anything to gain by keeping Indonesia in bondage, and time in which to "set the Indonesian free" was rapidly running out.

While these talks were going on at Terauchi's headquarters in Dalath near Saigon, the membership of the P.P.K.I. was announced.[16] It was to

---

12 Nishijima, Kishi, *et al., op. cit.*, p. 430.
13 Mohammad Hatta, "Legende dan Realiteit sekitar Proklamasi 17 Agustus" in Osman Raliby, ed., *Documenta Historica*, Lampiran, LXIV, p. 655.
14 As quoted in A. G. Pringgodigdo, *op. cit.*, p. 36.
15 See above, Chapter III, pp. 33-34 for an account of these sessions.
16 The membership of the P.P.K.I. was as follows:

Ir. Soekarno	Oto Iskandardinata
Drs. Mohammad Hatta	Abdul Kadir
Dr. Radjiman Wediodiningrat	R. Pandji Soeroso
Dr. Soepomo	M. Soetardjo Kartohadikoesoemo
Poeroebojo	Soerjohamidjojo
Wachid Hasjim	Ki Bagoes Hadikoesoemo
Dr. Mohammad Amir	Abdul Abbas
Tengkoe Mohd. Hasan	Dr. Ratulangie
Mr. Latuharhary	Andi Pangeran
I Goesti Ketoet Poetjo (Poedja)	
A. A. Hamidhan	Drs. Yap Tjwan Bing.

Cf. A. G. Pringgodigdo, *op. cit.*, p. 30, and *Soerara Moeslimin Indonesia*, III, # 16, (August 15, 1945), p. 1, The first 8 names represent secular nationalist and *prijaji* elements. Poeroebojo and Soerjohamidjojo were delegates for the principalities of Jogjakarta and Surakarta respectively. Wachid Hasjim and Hadikoesoemo represented the Islamic leadership. Abbas, Amir and Hasan, the three Sumatran delegates, were to speak for the Batak, Minang-kabau and Atjehnese areas, Ratulangie, Latuharhary, Andi Pangeran, Poedja and Hamidhan represented respectively Sulawesi-Christians, Moluccas-Christians, Sulawesi-non-Christians, Bali and Kalimantan. Drs. Yap Tjwan Bing was the delegate from the Chinese community.

have 21 members, divided geographically and ethnically as follows: Java 12, Sumatra 3, Sulawesi 2, Bali 1, Moluccas 1, Kalimantan 1, Chinese 1.[17] Mr, Subardjo was designated Advisor to the Committee.[18] By the time Soekarno, Hatta and Dr. Radjiman flew back to Djakarta on the 14th, Japan had effectively been brought to her knees by the horrors of Hiroshima and Nagasaki and Russia's entry into the war. After stopping off at Singapore to pick up the three Sumatran members of the P.P.K.I., the three leaders landed in Djakarta to be given an unprecedented welcome by the Commander of the 16th Army, General Nagano himself.

Soekarno, exultant over the success of the Saigon discussions and his sense of Indonesia's impending freedom, made a none too cryptic reference to the old Javanese legend of Djojobojo:[19]

> "If I used to say that Indonesia would only be free when the maize bore fruit, now I can declare that Indonesia will be free before it flowers!"

Later at a press interview, in answer to a question as to whether he had discussed the Constitution drawn up by the B.P.K.I. with Marshal Terauchi, he said:[20]

> "We certainly did not discuss it, since the problems of realizing our independence were unanimously handed over to us to solve,"

---

17 Aziz, *op. cit.*, p. 249, says 20 seats were reserved for Java, 4 for Sumatra and 4 for the Naval Territory, This is clearly wrong, but has its origin in the *Statement* of Nishimura, May 31-June 6, 1946, p. 4.

18 Mr. Soebardjo's appointment is listed in *Soeara Moeslimin Indonesia*, *loc. cit.*, and *Asia Raya*, August 14, 1945, but not in Pringgodigdo, *op. cit*. The P.P.K.I. 's administrative secretariat was headed by Hatta, with A. G. Pringgodigdo as his deputy, and Mr. Gondowardojo and Mr. Ismail Tajib as his assistants.

19 *Asia Raya*, August 14, 1945. For the legend of Djojobojo, cf. Tjantrik Mataram, *Peranan Ramalan Djojobojo dalam Revolusi Kita*, N. V."Masa Baru", Bandung, 1950. Also Pringgodigdo, op. cit., pp. 7f., and A. G. Pringgodigdo, *Tatanegara Djawa pada waktu pen-dudukan Djepang dari bulan Maret sampai bulan Desember 1942*, Jajasan Fonds Universitit Negeri Gadjah Mada, Jogjakarta, 1942, p. 11. The essence of the legend was that when the fortunes of Java were at their lowest, a yellow-skinned people from the North would occupy Java for a time equal to that taken by an ear of maize to ripen for harvest. Then they would leave, and Java would be free.

20 *Asia Raya*, August 16, 1945.

though he admitted that Indonesia would continue to accept Japan's leadership in the war, and would remain within the Greater East Asia Co-Prosperity Sphere.

CHAPTER SIX
THE INDEPENDENCE PROCLAMATION

It is probable that Hatta and Soekarno knew of Russia's entry into the war by the time they returned to Djakarta, and were reasonably sure that the fighting was unlikely to continue for more than a few weeks. Probably also they foresaw no insurmountable difficulties from the Japanese side. If anything the problem would be one of maintaining Indonesian discipline and unity. Hatta had spoken to Sjahrir, leader of the largest existing 'underground' organization, just prior to leaving for Saigon and Dalath. According to Sjahrir, he agreed that the time had come for a massive national effort, and that at Dalath, a very sharp line would have to be drawn between the Indonesian and Japanese positions, so that even the Indonesians who had "sincerely" collaborated would find themselves forced to join the Indonesian camp. Hatta also consented to Sjahrir's proposal to alert all branches of the various 'resistance' groups for action on his return.[1] Whether this report is wholly reliable or not,[2] Hatta himself reports that at 5:00 p. m. on the 14th he was visited by Sjahrir who told him that he was absolutely opposed to any independence that came as the gift of the Japanese.[3] He told Hatta that from its clandestine radios, his organization had heard that the Japanese Government had been putting out peace feelers since August 10th. The end of the war was clearly in sight; the arrival of the Allies was imminent. If Soekarno and Hatta declared independence at once, the "collaborationist" elements would

---

1 Sutan Sjahrir, *Out of Exile*, translated by Charles Wolf, Jr., John Day, N. Y., 1949, p, 253.
2 In view of his later strongly-expressed hostility towards "collaborationists "it is difficult to fathom his solicitude for such elements at this point. He must surely by this time have calculated that the only regime that stood a chance of Allied recognition would be one formed by unimpeachably anti-Japanese leaders.
3 Hatta, *op. cit.*, p. 656.

think that the declaration was the result of the Saigon talks, and would go along with it. Mass action could then be used against the Japanese Army. When the Allies arrived they would find a regime in power which had established itself by throwing off the Japanese yoke all on its own.

Sjahrir claims that Hatta was convinced by this reasoning, and merely-stipulated that no declaration without Soekarno's endorsement would have any effect, and that therefore he would have to try to persuade Soekarno as soon as possible. Sjahrir adds that Hatta agreed to abandoning the idea of using the P.P.K.I. to declare independence, as being too Japanized a body.[4] Hatta's account of this meeting places the emphasis rather differently. He apparently told Sjahrir that in his view the *means* of declaring independence were of no importance. If Soekarno was to be the man to declare it, it would make no difference as far as the Allies were concerned whether he did it on his own or through the P.P.K.I. He would still be viewed as a collaborator. Hatta then went to see Soekarno and found him quite unwilling to forego the P.P.K.I. He was not convinced that the Japanese were really on the verge of surrender, and wanted confirmation first from the Gunseikan, General Yamamoto.[5] There may however have been another reason for Soekarno's reluctance to abandon the P.P.K.I. The all-Indonesian representation on the Committee would in one sense make a declaration of independence more legitimate than any single man's proclamation could possibly be. Making use of the P.P.K.I. would also deprive the Japanese of a pretext for violent intervention. Both Soekarno and Hatta were worried that the underground and semi-underground youth groups would be unsuccessful in trying to overthrow the Japanese, and that there would be a useless bloodbath if an uprising were attempted.

In the meantime, Sjahrir, apparently convinced that Soekarno would declare independence, ordered all preparations set for the evening of the 15th. However, when Hatta returned to Sjahrir's house at noon that day, with the news of Soekarno's objections, Sjahrir persuaded him to go back with him to see Soekarno again. A long discussion ensued, the upshot being that Soekarno reportedly agreed to declare independence that

---

4 Sjahrir, *op. cit.*, p. 253.
5 Hatta, *op. cit.*, p. 656.

evening at 5:00 p. m. as Sjahrir had planned. Word was thereupon sent out to various key points on Java to prepare for the uprising. Thousands of Pemudas (youth activists) were to be assembled on the outskirts of Djakarta ready to be brought in by Peta trucks as soon as underground elements at the Djakarta radio station broadcast Soekarno's declaration. The immediate objectives of the *Pemudas* were to be the Military Police headquarters and the radio station. However matters did not develop as planned. At 6:00 p. m. word came from Soekarno that he would not go through with the plan and wanted to put off any move until the next day.[6] It is probable that the afternoon of the 15th was spent by the top official leadership in search of the key military officers who might be able to tell them how the situation in Japan was developing. But none was available. Only junior staff officers remained on the official premises. Accompanied by Soekarno, Hatta then proceeded to Maeda's. The Admiral told them he could give them no official word; but that in his opinion, the rumours circulating to the effect that Japan had surrendered were probably correct. In any case he would let them know if official word did come through.[7]

The two leaders then went home, prepared, according to Hatta, to issue invitations for a special meeting of the P.P.K.I. at 10:00 A.M. of the 16th, two days before that body's official inauguration was due. A short emergency meeting was envisaged at which the Declaration of Independence would be read out, and the Constitution briefly debated and adopted. A provisional government for Djakarta and the provinces would then be set up in the next few days, The members of the P.P.K.I. from outside Java would proceed to their home bases and set up provisional administrations, before the Japanese could surrender power to the Allies. For although Tokyo had agreed to independence, the Allies might be tempted to try to get the Japanese Army to maintain the *status quo ante* in Indonesia till they arrived.[8] If this account is correct, it does

---

6 Sjahrir, *op. cit.*, p. 255.
7 See *Statement* of Admiral Maeda, translated by S. Nishijima, April 16, 1947, p. 4, Maeda gives the interview as taking place at 3:00 p. m, on the 16th, but the date is a mistake. The two leaders were already at Rengasdengklok by the 16th, The Admiral must mean the 15th.
8 Hatta, *op. cit.*, p, 656, However, cf. also Sukarni Kartodiwirjo, "The 'Djakarta Charter' has no connection with the Proclamation of 17th August 1945," *Antara*, newsbulletin # 140/B, May 21, 1959, who avers that Hatta wanted the P.P.K.I. to meet only on August 23rd, as the Japanese had planned it.

much to explain why Soekarno changed his mind about Sjahrir's plans on the 15th. Thanks to Maeda's promise, a much less dangerous and equally rapid path to independence now seemed open. In the circumstances, it was unnecessary to risk a bloodbath.

In one sense however the change in policy came too late. Two youth leaders, Subadio and Subianto had arrived at Hatta's house at 5:00 p. m. that same day (the 15th) urging a *coup d'état* in Djakarta. Hatta refused to agree.[9] Communications between the various groups concerned seem at this point to have been very poor. The Sjahrir group appears to have been able to get news about Soekarno's intentions and activities only from Hatta, and even the usual emissaries between these two leaders were absent at this critical period. Whether through the reports of Subadio and Subianto, or by some other means, Sjahrir learnt of the change of plans, but too late to revoke his earlier orders everywhere, Dr. Sudarsono, leader of the Sjahrir organization in Tjirebon, had already begun an uprising there, which was promptly crushed, Sudarsono and some other leaders were arrested and jailed by the Kempeitai, At the same time Japanese suspicions in Djakarta were aroused by signs of unusual activity in the city and its environs. Several known underground leaders were arrested. And as the Kempeitai's armored cars patrolled the streets, tension steadily mounted.

A series of hurried and improvised meetings were held among the various underground organizations to adjust to the changing situation. Plans for surprising the Japanese were now clearly obsolete. The *coup d'état* was for the moment checkmated. Most of the younger people looked to Sjahrir to take the lead in declaring independence, but he rejected the idea, partly because Hatta's arguments on Soekarno's indispensability had convinced him, partly, it appears, because he was "still sure" that he could persuade Soekarno to act the following day.[10] It is not certain whether he knew of Hatta's plans for convening the P.P.K.I. the next morning, and if he did know, to what degree he approved or disapproved.

In any case, during the lull that followed the set-back to the scheduled uprising, word. came from certain underground contacts in the Japanese

---

9 Hatta, *op. cit.*, p. 657.
10 Sjahrir, *op. cit.*, p. 256; cf. also Kahin, *op. cit.*, pp. 134f.

administration that Japan had definitely surrendered.¹¹ The news provided the stimulus to some adventurous elements within the Menteng 31 and *Kaigun* youth groups, most notably Sukarni Kartodiwirjo, Chaerul Saleh, DjoharNoer, Subadio and Wikana, who were very dissatisfied with the way things were developing. In their eyes, it looked as if Sjahrir was being infected with the same hesitancy and dilatoriness that afflicted Soekarno and Hatta. Accordingly these elements, along with some members of the *Persatuan Mahasiswa*, assembled in the Bacteriological Laboratories behind the Medical school on Pegangsaan Timur to discuss the situation and make plans¹² According to Adam Malik, the meeting decided on an immediate declaration of independence "without any foreign participation." However some of those attending seem to have had misgivings, and on their urging, it was agreed to try to secure Soekarno's co-operation once more. Wikana and Darwis (one of Chaerul Saleh's associates) were chosen to carry a thinly-disguised ultimatum to him. The whole group would reassemble later that night to hear the results of the mission.¹³

At 10:00 p. m. of the 15th, Wikana and Darwis reached Soekarno's house and found him alone. Confronted with their demands for immediate action, Soekarno seems to have been in something of a quandary, though he firmly rejected the idea of acting till he received official word of the surrender from Yamamoto or Nishimura. He urged the youth groups to wait; independence was only a short step away. In any case, he told them that he could and would do nothing until he had consulted finally with Hatta and other senior nationalist leaders. The dispute became heated; the two youth leaders grew more and more upset that Soekarno continued to refuse to take the responsibility for declaring independence that night. Finally Wikana threatened that "If Bung Karno will not pronounce this

---

11 Probably the news came from Panduwiguna and Adam Malik who worked for the Domei radio network. The news of the surrender was not made generally public until August 21st, cf. *Asia Raya* of that date.
12 Adam Malik, *Riwajat dan Perdjuangan sekitar Proklamasi Kemerde-kaan Indonesia 17 Agustus 1945*, "Widjaja", Djakarta, 1950, p. 33. He adds the names of Kusnandar, Subianto, Aidit Sunjoto, Margono, Abubakar, Erie Sudewo and Armansjah. For a Communist version, see D. N. Aidit, *Pilihan Tulisan, 1951-1955*, Jajasan "Pembaruan", Djakarta, 1959, Vol. I., p. 508. He adds the names of Pardjono and Suroto Kunto.
13 Malik, *op. cit.*, p. 33. Aidit, *op. cit.*, *loc. cit.*, says Wikana, Aidit, Suroto Kunto and Subadio went to Soekarno's, with Wikana as their spokesman.

proclamation tonight, tomorrow there will be murder and bloodshed." At this Soekarno apparently became very angry, went over to Wikana and said: "Here is my throat! Drag me into the corner, and finish me off tonight! Don't wait till tomorrow." Wikana appears to have been somewhat abashed by this outburst, and merely repeated his warnings of a probable flare-up of popular violence.[14] Somehow Soekarno must have got word out as to what was going on, for Subardjo soon appeared at Hatta's house, urging him to go immediately to Pegangsaan Timur 56 where his colleague lived. Subardjo told Hatta that Soekarno was now surrounded by a gang of *pemudas* under the leadership of Wikana and Chaerul Saleh. Dropping the text of the Proclamation of Independence on which he had been working in preparation for the opening meeting of the P.P.K.I., Hatta hurried to the rescue with Subardjo.[15] On arrival at Soekarno's house, Hatta found argument still continuing, though by this time Dr. Buntaran Martoatmodjo and some other older nationalists had also arrived. Asked his opinion by Soekarno as to what course should now be taken, Hatta admitted that Sjahrir had already sent him word of the Japanese surrender, but that it was still "unofficial." He refused to act until he found out for certain what the attitude of the military authorities would be to any unauthorized declaration of independence.[16] He also gave the youth leaders a timely warning that neither he nor Soekarno would be pressured or coerced into doing anything rash, and sardonically challenged them to declare independence themselves if they thought they could carry it off. Wikana and Darwis were temporarily checked. They could only reply that "they would not answer for the consequences if the proclamation was not made the next morning at noon."[17]

What is clear from the accounts given by Malik and Hatta is that the most crucial question was one of timing. Hatta's story affirms his analysis of the whole Proclamation affair, the essence of which is that the younger and older leaders differed on *method*, not on timing. Both sides

---

14 Hatta, as quoted in *Fakta dan Dokumen*2, *op. cit.* p. 139.
15 Malik, *op, cit.*, p. 34.
16 *Ibid.* It is worth noting that Malik's book was written by a man generally regarded as politically opposed to both Sjahrir and Hatta in the post-revolutionary period.
17 *Ibid.* Cf. also Ali Moechtar Hoeta Soehoet, "Sedikit sekitar saat Lahirnja R. I. Proklamasi," M. D. Marpaung, ed., *op. cit.*, pp 28f. Aidit, *op. cit.*, p. 508, gives roughly the same story, only adding Iwa Kusumasumantri, Djojopranoto and Sudiro (mBah) to the list of those present.

wanted independence by the morning of the 16th. But the youth wanted a *putsch*, while the older leaders felt this to be unnecessary.[18] Malik however maintains that *timing*, as well as method was at stake. The older leaders had no intention of declaring independence until such time as the Japanese gave them permission.[19] If one accepts that Soekarno and Hatta had arranged for the P.P.K.I. to meet on the morning of the 16th (and it seems reasonable to do so), it is rather improbable that they would have failed to tell Wikana and Darwis of their plans. If one grants that the P.P.K.I. session had really been arranged, Malik's omission of any mention of it is to be explained either as deliberate suppression designed to discredit the older leaders, or due to Wikana and Darwis' having failed to pass the message on.

In any case, what emerges from both Hatta's and Malik's narratives, is that the older leaders had the stronger bargaining position. As Hatta said of the youth, "they had no leader of stature." Although in Malik's version the Wikana mission is depicted as the bold and triumphant issuing of an ultimatum, it is perhaps better seen as an astute bluff, designed to coerce the older nationalist leaders into immediate action. And the bluff was called. When challenged to declare independence themselves, the *pemuda* leaders could only retreat with vague threats and warnings. They still needed the older leaders. Though they had perhaps succeeded in stirring up a good deal of uncoordinated unrest in the city, they must have suspected, or sensed half-consciously, that without a national figure at their head (or a national figurehead) their uprising would be unsuccessful. An attempt to overthrow the Japanese regime in Djakarta would probably be crushed by forces moved in from the interior, unless the uprising could penetrate the other cities of Java and the rural hinterland. It must have been doubtful if this could be done rapidly by anyone but Soekarno and Hatta.

At about 11:30 p. m. of the 15th, Wikana and Darwis left for Tjikini 71 where the *pemuda* leaders had shifted their 'headquarters' to keep out of the clutches of the Kempeitai. At midnight, the second conference of the evening opened, under the chairmanship of Chaerul Saleh. As Malik describes it, it was decided that Soekarno and Hatta would have to be

---

18 Cf. Hatta, op. cit., p. 657."*Saja suka revolusi, akan tetapi menolak putsch.*" ("I want a revolution, not a putsch!'").
19 Malik, *op. cit.*, p. 35.

"evacuated" to a safe place outside Djakarta, where the "masses" and the Peta were ready "to face all possible consequences that might arise once independence was declared." Otherwise, "if Bung Karno-Hatta were to remain in the city, they could be made use of by the Japanese to crush or obstruct the Independence Proclamation."[20]

It is difficult to be sure how to interpret this claim. It is possible that the *pemudas* were really convinced that the older leaders were too timid to declare independence without Japanese approval, and were really afraid that after the surrender this approval would never be given. On the other hand there was as yet no indication that the Japanese had changed their minds about going through with their own brand of independence. And they would probably think twice before arresting Soekarno and Hatta, an act which might set off a dangerous reaction among the Indonesian masses. It is perhaps most likely that the attitude of the *pemuda* leaders represented an attempt to maintain the momentum of their earlier activities, and to make good the bluff that Soekarno and Hatta had just called. As the events of the next day were to prove, "evacuating" Soekarno and Hatta out of Djakarta was simply a renewal of the first ultimatum, more imposing but hardies less hollow. The *pemudas* perhaps gambled that once outside Djakarta, the psychological atmosphere would be such that Soekarno and Hatta would yield to their demands. But the net result of their reactions was a delay in the attainment of their ostensible goals. And the fact that none of the '*pemuda*' accounts claims that an uprising in Djakarta was attempted *while the older leaders were outside the city*, tends to support this interpretation. The youth needed Soekarno and Hatta to lead the revolution, not to stop the Japanese from using them to crush it.

Malik's story that the decision to "evacuate" Soekarno and Hatta was taken by a unanimous vote of the whole youth conference at Tjikini 71, is to some degree contradicted by the testimony of Sjahrir. Sjahrir reports that he was only told about the conference at 1:00 A.M. that morning, and that at 2:00 A.M. (of the 16th) some delegates from the meeting came to him suggesting that only by kidnapping Soekarno and Hatta could the objectives of the underground groups be attained. Sjahrir however replied that it would be unnecessary since he was sure he could control

---

20 *Ibid., loc. cit.*

the situation by contacting Soekarno the next day. The young men left, only to return an hour later with the news that "a clique in the assemblage" had, contrary to the consensus, kidnapped the two leaders.[21] Neither account is entirely satisfactory. Perhaps a more plausible hypothesis is that two meetings really took place: First, a large and heterogeneous gathering of all groups, including members of Sjahrir's organization, heard Wikana's account of his mission and its failure. Then the idea of kidnapping Soekarno and Hatta was perhaps mooted. Sjahrir's support was then solicited, but his rejection of the idea settled the matter for the majority of the members, who thereupon dispersed. Then, after the main conference broke up, a second conference was held by such like-minded spirits as Sukarni, Wikana and Chaerul Saleh. This smaller group decided to go ahead with the kidnapping plans, and so re-assume the initiative. Responsibility was divided, with Sukarni in charge of the actual operation, Singgih, from the Peta, detailed to handle liaison with friendly Peta groups, and Chaerul Saleh and Wikana left behind in Djakarta to watch the course of events, spy on the Japanese and, in time, to warn other *pemudas* of their *fait accompli*.[22]

Whatever the case, the conspirators, Sukarni, Chaerul Saleh, Singgih, J. Kunto and Dr. Muwardi (of the *Barisan* Pelopor), proceeded to the house of D. Asmoro, another member of their group, to pick up a second car. With their two cars, they managed to evade *Kempeitai* patrols and appear at the houses of Soekarno and Hatta sometime between 4:00 and 4:30 a.m.[23] The two nationalist leaders were roused from their beds, and forced, along with Soekarno's wife and infant son, to accompany the *pemudas*. In spite of Soekarno's protests and arguments, the two cars were driven past the Japanese watchposts to the Peta barracks at Rengasdengklok, some 30 miles outside Djakarta in the direction of Tjirebon.[24] The area had previously been one of unrest and anti-Japanese

---

21 Sjahrir, op. cit., pp. 256f. On p. 257 however Sjahrir says that the kidnapping took place on the morning of the 15th — which is certainly wrong — and that the final declaration of independence was made in Admiral Maeda's house on the morning of the 16th, which is also incorrect. There are other vagaries in his account.
22 Malik, op. cit., pp. 36-38, Also Ali Moechtar Hoeta Soehoet, op. cit., in D. Marpaung, ed., op. cit., p. 31.
23 As a historical curiosity, it is interesting that Sukarni and Muwardi were involved in the kidnapping of Prime Minister Sjahrir on June 27, 1946.
24 Aidit, op. cit., p. 508 names Sukarni, Kunto, Muwardi, Singgih and Sutjipto as kidnappers. For

activity. It was within easy reach of the capital, and advantageously situated to dominate Krawang and Tjikampek, and guard the road and railway into Djakarta from Tjirebon and Purwakarta.

The Peta Battalion commander at Purwakarta was warned by two of the conspirators, Singgih and Dr. Sutjipto, acting as liaison men, that the two leaders were on their way. On the orders of the local company commander at Rengasdengklok, Subeno, who had previously had extensive contacts with the Menteng 31 group through Sutjipto, the whole area surrounding the Peta barracks was sealed off. The village of Rengasdengklok was put under "Republican" martial law and guards were set up on all roads leading to the village and barracks to warn against any Japanese countermeasures. At noon of the 16th, the Resident of Djakarta,[25] Sutardjo, was arrested just as he was returning from the capital, where he had gone to attend the scheduled inauguration of the P.P.K.I.[26] The local wedana (district officer), Abdurrachman, and several other local officials suspected of being Japanese agents were also arrested. The *tjamat* (sub-district officer), Hadipranoto, a known Republican, was put in temporary charge of civilian affairs. To all appearances, the operation was carried out with speed and efficiency, and without the Japanese suspecting what was in the wind.

On their arrival, Soekarno and Hatta were taken to the house of a local Chinese trader, I Song, and there kept under guard. There seems to have been a lot of arguing and vehement discussion, but neither side was willing to budge.[27] As the day wore on however, the psychological advantage began to shift to the older leaders. Resident Sutardjo told Sukarni that he had gone to the previously arranged meeting of the P.P.K.I., and had been amazed when Soekarno and Hatta had not appeared.[28] It was obvious

---

further details of the actual kidnapping, see Malik, *op. cit.*, pp. 36-38.
25 The Residency of Djakarta did not include the city of Djakarta itself.
26 Bachsan, *op. cit.*, p, 49. Malik, *op. cit.*, p. 39, says Sutardjo was leaving *for* the capital, and says nothing about the P.P.K.I. meeting, but Bachsan's report looks more likely, partly because he has no obvious axe to grind, Cf. also Aidit, *op. cit.*, p. 508. Ali Moechtar Soehoet, *op. cit.*, in D. Marpaung, ed., *op. cit.*, pp. 3 If., says that arrangements had been made long before. Between them Singgih, Bachsan, the local section commander, and Sujono Hadipranoto, the local *tjamat*, had long planned for a declaration of independence on the 16th. Although to some extent corroborated by Bachsan, *op. cit.*, pp. 38-48, the story seems unlikely. The whole kidnapping alfair gives a strong impression of last-minute improvisation.
27 Bachsan, *op. cit.*, p. 50. Malik, *op. cit.*, p. 40.
28 Bachsan, *op. cit.*, p. 49.

therefore that the Japanese would now be hunting for them add their kidnappers. There was no way that Sukarni could force Soekarno and Hatta to yield, or, in fact, to publicize a declaration of independence if they had yielded. It was becoming apparent that the plan had been rashly conceived, and was likely to prove fruitless. Kahin relates that Sukarni did manage to persuade Soekarno and Hatta that Japan had surrendered, but that his claim that there were 15, 000 armed *pemudas* ready outside Djakarta waiting to seize power, was received sceptically. Both were convinced that some arrangement could be made with the Japanese.[29] In any event, about noon of the 16th, Sukarni decided to send Kunto back to Djakarta to find out how the land lay, and to contact the conspirators there, probably Chaerul Saleh and Wikana.[30]

Meanwhile in Djakarta, the Japanese were busy. At noon on the 15th, the Army Information Department had heard the Surrender messages delivered in Tokyo by Prime Minister Suzuki and the Emperor.[31] The official telegram however did not arrive until midnight, just about the time the youth conference was being held at Tjikini 71. On the morning of the 16th, Admiral Maeda took steps to warn Soekarno and Hatta, as he had promised. But the two leaders were nowhere to be found. Maeda immediately suspected that the *Kempeitai* had arrested them, in order to nip an uprising in the bud. But when he went to Army Headquarters, he found them as mystified as he was,[32] Nishimura later testified that though he had been warned by Soekarno of the danger that the youth represented, he had not thought to do more than have the radio-station carefully guarded. On the morning of the 16th, however, a Mr. Terada, Hatta's 'secretary,' called in to say that Hatta 's family had reported that he had been out all night and was not yet back. Nishimura then heard from Yamamoto, who had been conferring with Maeda, about the disappearance of the two leaders.[33] It was now becoming clear that the

---

29 Kahin, *op. cit.*, p. 135. However it should be noted that Hatta claims that he had already been convinced of the truth of the surrender reports, and, as we have seen, his statement that the P.P.K.I. was due to meet on the 16th is supported independently by the episode of Resident Sutardjo. Cf. Hatta, *op. cit.*, p. 656, and Bachsan, *ibid.*
30 Malik, *op. cit.*, p. 43.
31 Cf. *Statement* of Captain Kiso Tsuchiya of the Beppan, April 3-8, 1947, p. 7.
32 *Statement* of Admiral Maeda, April 16, 1947, p. 4.
33 *Statement* of Nishimura, April 25. 1947, pp. 1f. Apparently the Army was very angry and upset at not being able to trace the two leaders. Cf. also Nishijima, Kishi, *et al.*, *op. cit.*, p. 495.

only people who could have kidnapped Soekarno and Hatta were the *pemuda* elements. It was not however so clear that the act had been done without the connivance of the "victims." Maeda was now receiving reports that there were at least 6, 000 *pemudas* in Djakarta prepared for a *coup d'état*,[34] The situation was very delicate. The Japanese, conscious of their position as a defeated army, were loath to do anything that might unnecessarily cause unrest. In view of the tense psychological atmosphere and the mood of the *pemudas*, an attempt to get Soekarno and Hatta back by force could be the spark that would set the dry stubble of Indonesian nationalism alight.

Apparently Yamamoto, Nishimura and Maeda decided that more diplomatic methods were called for.[35] Maeda instructed his aide Nishijima to try and find out what he could through the *Kaigun* organization. Nishijima thereupon hurried off to track down Wikana at his home. After some hours of discussion and pleading Nishijima got Wikana to reveal that plans had been made for seizing the radio station that night, and using it to declare independence all over Java immediately. In the meantime, Soekarno and Hatta were in the charge of some "comrades." Nishijima then told Wikana that he and Maeda had no objection to an independence proclamation that night (the 16th), but that the P.P.K.I. was the appropriate instrument. A *coup d'état* without the presence and leadership of Soekarno and Hatta would be foolhardy in the extreme. Wikana's suspicions seem partly to have been overcome, and he agreed to consult his comrades, The result of the consultations appears to have been that the *pemudas* in Djakarta were willing to allow Soekarno and Hatta to return to Djakarta, on the condition that the personal safety of all parties was guaranteed by Admiral Maeda. Wikana however insisted in the meantime on keeping the location of the two leaders secret, to protect his group from possible Japanese double-dealing. Nishijima thereupon called on the services of Mr. Subardjo, acting head of the *Asrama Indonesia Merdeka*, for

---

34 *Statement* of Admiral Maeda, April 16, 1947, p. 4. Maeda said: "I felt that the coup was much more serious than the disappearnce of Soekarno-Hatta. If they (the youth) tried a coup, it would mean fighting with the Japanese Army. civil war and bloodshed.... The first job was to get Soekarno-Hatta back....on the condition that their return would be temporary and under Indonesian auspices."

35 *Statement* of Maeda, April 16, 1947, p. 4. Maeda comments: "All the time I kept the Gunseikan (Yamamoto) informed of progress. Precautions had meantime been taken by the Army."

a delicate diplomatic mission. He was to go with two of Wikana's people to the place where Soekarno, Hatta and their kidnappers were hiding, and try to bring them back to Djakarta. Subardjo agreed to go provided that Maeda guaranteed that Independence would be declared that night, and that none of the youth leaders would be punished. These conditions Maeda accepted, and promised that, if necessary, the Indonesians could use his house (which had quasi- 'extraterritorial' status vis-a-vis the Japanese Army) as a meeting place.[36]

The problem was basically how to bridge the gap between the kidnappers and the Japanese Army, and find some solution which could satisfy all parties and cause none of them to lose too much face or seriously endanger their positions. An elaborate and extended chain of communication was thus constructed running through Yamamoto, Maeda, Nishijima, Subardjo, Wikana and Sukarni, with each link a little more 'trusted' by the Rengasdengklok group. It was a situation where brokers were badly needed. Subardjo was excellently equipped to play this role, though it should be realized that under the tense circumstances his mission might well have failed, and himself been killed, or at least hopelessly compromised politically, had the Japanese failed to live up to their promises.

Accordingly in the late afternoon of the 16th, about 5:00 p. m., Subardjo set out for Rengasdengklok, accompanied by Sudiro and Kunto, who had been Sukarni's messenger to Wikana.[37] On arrival at Rengasdengklok, Subardjo was apparently received with a good deal of suspicion, until he convinced Sukarni that he had really come at Wikana's request, that the

---

36 Nishijima, Kishi et al., op. cit., pp. 495ff. Cf. Nishijima's *Verklaring betreffende deindonesische Onafhankelijkheidsbeweging en de Bijeenkomsten ten huize van Maeda op 16/17 Augustus 1945*, deposed before Military Auditor A. P. M. Audretsch, March 10-13, 1947, pp. 3ff., for a more detailed (and self-effacing) account of the role of the *Kaigun* office at this time. Both accounts emphasize the importance and patriotism of Mr. Subardjo in this affair. Cf. also H. J. de Graaf, "The Indonesian Declaration of Independence," *Bijdragen tot de Taal-, Land- en Volkenkunde*, Deel 115, 1959, pp. 317ff.

37 In his answers to *Supplementary Questions*, of April 16, 1947, p. 1, Maeda claimed that his aide Yoshizumi went along too. This is not corroborated by any Indonesian source except perhaps Sjahrir, who writes (*op. cit.*, p. 257) that he made a surprise visit to a highly-placed Indonesian collaborator who told him that there had been no mass arrests, owing to the intervention of "his Japanese Naval friends. A leading Indonesian collaborator and a Japanese" had been sent out to Rengasdengklok to negotiate for the prisoners' release. The story seems unlikely in view of Subardjo's already delicate and ambiguous situation.

surrender was now official, and that all preparations for a declaration of independence in Djakarta had now been made.[38] Subardjo's arrival showed Soekarno and Hatta that the Japanese either already knew or shortly would know all about the youths' plans, and they were thus even more convinced that a coup would fail, now that the element of surprise had been removed. For some hours Subardjo's offer was debated, and three-way negotiations between Soekarno-Hatta, Sukarni, and Subardjo were thrashed out. Finally the offer was accepted by all parties. Soekarno, Hatta and Sukarni agreed to go back with Subardjo to Djakarta. The proclamation would be made that night, probably in Maeda 's house. The personal security of all parties was guaranteed by Subardjo.[39] Soekarno and Hatta were sure that Subardjo, being a close associate of Maeda 's, was telling the truth about the surrender, and knew enough of Maeda's views and personality (and influence) to believe in his sincerity. It is less easy to assess Sukarni's attitude. He had previously been well-acquainted with Subardjo, and so must have realized that the *Kaigun* office was behind Subardjo's mission, and possibly even that the Japanese Army was involved. One cannot help thinking that he was glad to have someone else take the initiative and allow him to emerge from the impasse into which he had been driven.

By 11:00 p. m. of the 16th, all the protagonists of Rengasdengklok had arrived back in Djakarta. On leaving the barracks, Sukarni had reportedly whispered to Bachsan, the section commander in charge, to "go ahead with the revolution" if he did not return, but this was now merely a gesture. For the moment everything lay in Maeda's hands. And to his house on the old Oranje-Nassau Boulevard they all proceeded.[40]

---

38 Cf. *Statement* of Maeda, April 16, 1947, p. 4. For further details see S. Nishijima's *Verklaring*, pp. 4ff., and Malik, *op. cit.*, pp. 44f. However Hatta's comment that Subardjo came as *"utusan Gunseikanbu"* (emissary of the Gunseikan's office) may mean that Malik's version on which this analysis is based is wrong, and that Subardjo's role was quite explicit *at the time*. See Hatta, *op. cit.*, p. 657.

39 Doubtless the main arguments took place between Sukarni and Subardjo. This may account for the fact that Hatta's account mentions no discussions, in fact denies that any took place, See Hatta, *loc. cit.* For a splendid, if highly stylized and theatrical account of the debate at Rengasdengklok, see Tan Malakka, *op. cit.*, pp. 56ff. He claims that a deal was made whereby in exchange lor a promise to declare independence between 6:00 A.M. and 12:00 noon on the 17th, Soekarno was able to get the youth to agree to take no action till his time was up. Unfortunately he also says (p. 57), that Subardjo persuaded Soekarno to declare independence that night at 10:00 p. m.!

40 Nishijima, Kishi *et al*, *op. cit.*, p. 497.

On their arrival Maeda immediately telephoned General Yamamoto and asked him to attend the meeting, The Gunseikan however refused and told Maeda to see Nishimura — and in any case to take no action until the morning.[41] Soekarno, Hatta and Maeda then agreed, over the protests of the *pemuda* representatives, that they should try to find Nishimura, and at least secure his neutrality. Shortly after midnight, they hurried to his residence, where he was sitting up waiting for them, having been warned earlier of a possible visit by both Maeda and Yamamoto. Nishimura afterwards described the meeting in these terms:[42]

> "Soekarno and Hatta together visited me with Rear-Admiral Maeda.. Soekarno and Hatta demanded immediate independence. Whereupon Rear-Admiral Maeda asked them from his heart of hearts to behave prudently, while, endeavouring to drive their attention to the Japanese standpoint, I also persuaded them for long hours not to take any unlawful steps, ignoring the Japanese ground (sic). Upon this occasion they requested furthermore to open the Preparatory Committee for Independence1 immediately on the 17th, but I stubbornly refused to accept this proposal saying to the effect that I had no right to acknowledge that sort of proposal whatever, This strong rejection won them to consent, as they had known that the meeting of the conference was expected to be held on the 18th. On the other hand, however, both Messrs, Soekarno and Hatta were so much excited, and, therefore, Rear-Admiral Maeda left my house with them, while soothing them down."

The meeting was obviously hardly a success. However Maeda remained calm, and seems to have had the situation well in hand. Nishimura claims that when the three men left, he had no suspicion that Maeda was going to help them declare independence, but thought he was just going to calm them down."When they left my house. I only believed that they were going to the Maeda's (sic) for being appeased by Admiral Maeda (But) when leaving my house they were excited, so I had some suspicion on their

---

41 *Ibid.*, p. 498.
42 *Statement* of Nishimura, April 15, 1947, pp. 1f, Cf. Aziz, *op. cit.*, p. 256, for an exceedingly free version of the same passage.

action to come. I ordered Mr. Miyoshi to get further information about them, and asked Mr. Miyano, the Chief of Police. to get prepared for the emergency cases which might happen."[43] Miyano saw to it that a strong guard was stationed at the radio-station and the printing presses.[44]

Maeda avers that there was a representative of the Gunseikan present in his house on the night of the l6th.[45] A Dutch source states that:[46]

> "Nishimura and his people did not dare to send along an official person, because they knew Soekarno's mentality. He could make political capital by saying this meant the assemblage was approved of by the Gunseikan's office, which was represented there, and ratified its decisions. Yet they still felt obliged to find out what did go on and so sent an interpreter, who got drunk and fell asleep at Maédás."

No Indonesian source except Tan Malakka confirms the presence of Japanese officials at Maeda's on the night of the 16th. It seems reasonable to suppose that at this point the Japanese were prepared to turn a blind eye on Maeda's activities, and while unwilling to assume the responsibility for independence, were not at this stage unhappy to see it take place, symbolically at least. For so long as they controlled the means of communication on Java, the practical consequences of a quiet Declaration in Maeda's house were not likely to prove dangerous. Moreover the fact that the declaration had been made might temper the impatience and restlessness of the *pemudas* in Djakarta. Moreover if the

---

43 *Statement* of Nishimura, April 25, 1947, p. 2. Cf. also *ibid.*, p. 4.
44 Cf. de Graaf, *op. cit.*, pp. 321f. for a rather different account, which emphasizes Nishimura 's refusal to take any initiative till he received orders from above, and his refusal to allow a P.P.K.I. meeting, though a private "tea-party" at Soekarno's would not be prevented. This charge however is firmly rejected by Nishimura himself, see his Statement of April 25, 1947, p. 1.
45 *Statement* of Maeda, April 16, 1947, p. 5, In his answers to *Supplementary Questions*, April 16, 1947, p, 1, Maeda added that Yoshizumi was also present, as well as Saito, Nakatani and Miyoshi, all from the Political Section of the Department of General Affairs. Nishijima, in his *Verklaring*,. p. 8, says that Miyoshi was asked along at Maeda's request as a representative of the Gunseikan's office to give the meeting an "official" aura. He also avers, contrary to Nishimura, that Nishimura had agreed to move up the inauguration of the P.P.K.I. one day to the 18th, on Soekarno's and Hatta's urgings.
46 E. Brunsveld van Hulten, *Rapport over de Japansche Invloed op de Merdekabeweging en de Gebeurtenissen in de Augustdagen*, July 24, 1946. p. 7.

Army wished to sit on the fence and blur its responsibilities, it was good sense to send along a civilian employee of the Gunseikan's office in an unofficial capacity.[47]

Meanwhile Sukarni, who had been left behind at Maeda's with Nishi jima and the others "suddenly remembered" that certain plans had been laid for a violent military uprising in Djakarta that very night. What this "uprising" amounted to is rather obscure. According to Malik, Chaerul Saleh, the brains behind the scheme, had already on August 15th set about organizing a conference of favorably-inclined Peta officers and leaders in the *Seinendan* and *Barisan Pelopor*. Among these were Dr. Muwardi of the *Barisan Pelopor* and Company Commander Abdul La tief, temporarily in charge of the Djakarta Peta garrison, in the absence of Battalion Commander Kasman Singodimedjo.[48] The meeting was actually held on the morning of the 16th, soon after Sukarni, Soekarno and Hatta had left for Rengasdengklok, in the billiard-room of the Zoological Gardens. At the meeting it was decided that:[49]

1. The Peta and Heiho units were to lead the attack on the Japanese in Djakarta.
2. *Pemudas* and students who had had military training and knew how to handle weapons would be issued arms from the Peta arsenals, and taken by truck to the city limits to wait there as reserves till they were needed.
3. A detailed study of Japanese barracks and guardposts, already being carried on by the students, would be continued, and the results passed on to the Peta commanders.

---

47 Cf. for a different interpretation of Maeda's and Nishimura's actions at this point, De Graaf, *op. cit.*, p. 322.
48 See an article by Nawawi Dusky in *Harian Abadi*, August 22, 1955, for a favorable account of Kasman's role in the Proclamation Affair. Nawawi claims that Kasman knew about the surrender on the 15th, and when invited to Bandung that day by the Japanese authorities, he expected that they would hand over military power to him. He was then unpleasantly surprised to find that this was not the case. His zealous patriotism however was demonstrated by the fact that "it was in Kasman's truck that Soekarno and Hatta were taken to Rengasdengklok!" No mention is made of the proposed *pemuda* uprising, or of Chaerul Saleh's organization. For a *pemuda* view of his role, see Malik, op. cit., pp. 41-43. It should be remembered however that as a Battalion Commander, Kasman's job in the Peta was more political than military, involving mostly liaison work with the *Djawa Hookookai*.
49 Malik, *op. cit.*, pp. 41f.

4. All action would be directed by the Peta and Heiho headquarters.
5. The uprising would start at 1:00 A.M. on August 17th.
6. Village units would be directed by local leaders towards assisting the military action.
7. Communications, codes and passwords would be agreed on.

Malik claims that the students actually carried out their assigned reconnoitring operations, and reported to the "coup" headquarters then stationed at Prapatan 10. But at 8:15 p.m. that evening (the 16th) word came from Kasman Singodimedjo that the Peta and Heiho would not move without orders from Soekarno.[50] This upset the *pemudas*' plans completely. Chaerul Saleh and his group appear to have believed that as Kasman knew that Soekarno was still at Rengasdengklok in Peta hands, his message could only mean that he had lost his nerve and was retreating from his commitments. A student mission was sent out to find him, but to no avail.[51]

However another aspect of Malik's account appears to conflict with this story. He records that early in the evening of the 16th, Wikana had succeeded in extracting from the Menteng group a promise that they would not move until he had heard the results of Subardjo's mission to Rengasdengklok that afternoon. When they had heard Wikana's explanation of the situation, the group broke up (at 8:40 p. m.), agreeing to reconvene at 10:00 p. m. when the news from Subardjo should have come through.[52] The second story seems the more convincing. The time interval between the report of Kasman's defection, 8:15 p. m., and the *break-up* of the youth conference after Wikana's report at 8:45 is too short to be convincing, especially as part of the conference agreement was to postpone action till word came from Subardjo. If the Kasman story is correct, 'action' must have been out of the question by 8:15 or shortly

---

50 Malik, *op. cit.*, p. 42.
51 Dr. Sutjipto, who, as a Peta Company Commander, acted as liaison between Chaerul Saleh's group and the Peta garrisons in Djakarta and its environs, seems to have been overwhelmed by Kasman's message. He said to an angry Chaerul Saleh: "I don't understand Kasman and Latief. God knows where they've got to now. For you civilians it's not so bad, but for us, who've been glorified with the name of Defenders of the Fatherland, to fail in our duty, hiii, hiii!" Malik, *ibid.*, *loc. cit.*
52 Malik, *op. cit.*, pp. 43f.

thereafter anyway. In any case, morale among the *pemudas* must have been temporarily low. Djohar Noer had told the conference that attempts to penetrate Japanese guards at Radio Djakarta had failed. The atmosphere was gloomy and tense. The *Kempeitai* seemed everywhere in control.[53]

Nevertheless, certain pemuda elements had agreed that in case Sukarni, Soekarno and Hatta did not re-appear in Djakarta by 12:00 midnight, they would attempt an uprising.[54] In any case such an attempt would have been rash. But with Soekarno's and Hatta's return to the capital, it might well have been disastrous. The delicate compromise engineered by Maeda, Nishijima and Subardjo would have collapsed in ruins if fighting broke out in the streets. The Army's hitherto hesitant and equivocal attitude would have hardened into murderous hostility. Sukarni's belated recollection of the scheduled uprising meant that action had to be taken immediately. Nishijima and Sukarni thereupon set off to warn the *pemudas* to hold their hand. The car stopped at key points on Djalan Tjikini and behind the Pasar Senen, as well as Chaerul Saleh's temporary headquarters at Prapatan 10. To the clusters of *pemudas* gathered on street-corners and in alleyways Sukarni called his warning: "*Ini hari tidak djadi, bung,*" (Not today, brother!) Some of the youths must have been hard to persuade, or suspicious of Sukarni's Japanese riding companion. Nishijima reports Sukarni climbing back wearily into the car muttering: "*Mereka ini semuanja kepala batu, susah!*" (What a pig-headed lot they all are!)[55] The last and most crucial spot was the radio station on the Koningsplein, which was supposed to be the main target of the *pemudas*' onslaught. They found it heavily guarded by the *Kempeitai*, and were immediately arrested. Only when a telephone call was put through to Maeda were they

---

53 Malik, *op. cit.*, p. 43. Cf. also Aidit, *op. cit*, p. 508. He agrees with Malik that the *pemudas*, and certain Peta and Heiho elements planned a coup. Those assigned to the key task of mobilizing "the people of Djakarta" were Aidit, Lukman, Sidik Kertapati, Suko, Gundiwan Muljono, Njono, Samsuddin, A.M. Hanafi, etc. Plans were simultaneously made for spreading the word of the Proclamation and seizing independence in the "regions" (*daerah2*). The crucial meeting for this purpose was held at 4:00 p. m of the 16th (i. e. as Kunto arrived in Djakarta from Rengasdengklok), at Armunanto's house on Gang Sentiong. Present were: Sidik Djojo-sukarto, Widarta, Kartopandojo, Sujono, Sudiro (mBah), Inu Kertapati, Sundoro, Ukon Effendi and Armunanto himself. Aidit attributes the collapse of the coup to insufficient preparation, the lack of a firm revolutionary core in the Peta leadership (i. e. Kasman and Latief), and poor coordination between revolutionary groups within Djakarta and those outside.
54 Nishijima, *Verklaring.*, March 10-13, 1947, p. 6.
55 *Ibid.*, pp. 6f.

both released. Finally with their mission successfully accomplished, they returned to Maeda's house.[56]

While Nishijima and Sukarni had been busy forestalling an uprising, and Maeda, Soekarno and Hatta had been conferring with Nishimura, Mr. Subardjo had been active, on instructions from Hatta, in routing as many members of the P.P.K.I. as possible out of their beds, and bringing them to Maeda's house. By the time the Admiral and his two companions returned, many of these had already arrived. It was at this point, according to Kahin, that Sjahrir visited Soekarno and "elicited from him a promise to declare independence; however, he was unable to secure from him a commitment that it would be done in the strongly anti-Japanese terms that he and his group advocated."[57] Sjahrir himself merely says that a delegation arrived asking him to attend the signing of the Proclamation, and that he refused because he was sure that the proclamation finally issued would not run along the same lines as the one he had prepared himself. In any case a revolutionary document could hardly be signed at the house of a Japanese admiral.[58] There can be little doubt, even discounting Malik's polemical analysis, that he is right in saying that the initiative had passed out of Sjahrir's hands, and that in these three historic days, he remained largely a spectator. Indeed he admits as much himself. With the Menteng and *Kaigun* groups now at least partially co-operating with the older leaders and the Japanese, the "anti-Fascist" revolt he had dreamed of seemed rather remote.

There is a good deal of controversy as to who actually attended the final meeting at Maeda's when the Proclamation of Independence was drafted and signed. Although all Indonesian sources except Tan Malakka deny that any Japanese were present, we have it on the generally reliable authority of Nishijima that he, Maeda, Yoshizumi and Miyoshi were on hand, at least for some of the time.[59] It is certainly unlikely that having played so important a part in setting the stage for independence, they

---

56 Nishijima, *Verklaring,.*, March 10-13, 1947, p. 7. Cf. also the interesting account of Hasjim Mahdan in *Indonesia Raya*, August 16, 1955. As one of the *Pemudas* attached to Prapatan 10, he was assigned to the job of taking over this radio station, for the all-important task of publicizing independence. See also Maeda's answers to *Supplementary Questions*, April 16, 1947, p 1.
57 Kahin, *op. cit.*, p. 136.
58 Sjahrir, *op. cit.*, p. 258.
59 Nishijima, Kishi *et al.*, *op. cit.*, p. 499f.

would be content to vanish entirely from the scene. It is perhaps worth noting that in the immediate post-Independence period, an admission of even minor Japanese participation would have been damaging in Allied eyes, and this consideration perhaps allows one to regard Indonesian treatments of this point with some reservations.

Hatta says simply that all the members of the P.P.K.I. and the leaders of some "youth"and other organizations met together and accepted a suggestion by the youth leaders that the proclamation should be signed by Soekarno and Hatta alone.[60] Sjahrir agrees that all the P.P.K.I. members attended, and adds that they called themselves a National Committee for the occasion.[61] Kahin lists all the members of the P.P.K.I. as well as Subardjo, Sukarni and Wikana.[62] Pringgodigdo believes that not all the P.P.K.I. representatives attended, as it was late at night; on the other hand such youth leaders as Sukarni, Chaerul Saleh, and B.M. Diah, and some older nationalists like Dr. Buntaran and Semaun Bakri were present.[63] A.M. Hoeta Soehoet and Malik list B.M. Diah, Semaun Bakri, Sajuti Melik (just out of jail), Iwa Kusumasumantri, Sukarni, Subardjo, and Chaerul Saleh, as well as Soekarno and Hatta.[64] Dimyati, who claims to follow the main lines of Malik's account of the Proclamation affair, gives as present:[65]

*Soekarno	*Hatta	*Subardjo	*Soetardjo
*Latuharhary	*Dr. Amir	*Dr. Radjiman	*Dr. Soepomo
*Iskandardinata	*Poedja	*Hamidhan	*A. Abbas

---

60 Hatta, op. cit., p. 657.
61 Sjahrir, op. cit., p. 258.
62 Kahin, op. cit., p. 136.
63 A. G. Pringgodigdo, Perubahan Kabinet Presidensil Mendjadi Kabinet Parlementer, Jajasan Fonds Universitit Negeri Gadjah Mada, Jog-Jakarta, no date, p. 17.
64 A.M. Hoeta Soehoet, in D. Marpaung, ed., op. cit., p. 33. Malik, op. cit., p. 51. Malik says that Sukarni, Iwa, Subardjo, and Kunto left together for Djalan Bogor Lama, the new pemuda headquarters, and after discussions there, accepted Sukarni and Chaerul Saleh as pemuda spokesmen. He adds that Sjahrir was there, and concurred. Tan Malakka, op. cit., p. 59 agrees, and adds that Sukarni and Chaerul Saleh were chosen by a group including Sjahrir, Maruto, Panduwiguna, Adam Malik, Kusnaeni and Djawoto. It is curious that in Malik's list the P.P.K.I. is not mentioned at all, and that those honourably cited there were all eventually to join Malik as members of Tan Malakka's Persatuan Perdjuangan.
65 M. Dimyati, Sedjarah Perdjuangan Indonesia, Widjaja, Djakarta, 1951, p. 90. The names with asterisks are those of members of the P.P.K.I.

*Moh. Hasan	*Ratulangie		*Andi Pangeran
Dr. Buntaran	Dr. Samsi	A.A. Rivai	Iwa Kusumasumantri
			Andi Sultan Daeng Radja,

"and various other youth and revolutionary leaders." Tan Malakka concurs and adds Supeno, Gunadi, Semaun Bakri, Sajuti Melik, B.M. Diah, Kunto, Chaerul Saleh, Sukarni, as well as Maeda, Nishijima, Miyoshi and Saito.[66]

If we combine Dimyati's and Tan Malakka's accounts, we find a good sprinkling of youth leaders, older nationalists, and 15 of the 22 members of the P.P.K.I., which seems very reasonable for that hour of the night. It also squares with Nishijima's figure of about 30 people being present, "mainly members of the P.P.K.I. and older nationalists living in Djakarta"[67]

The substance of the long and heated discussion that followed was the content of the Independence Proclamation. Sjahrir's proposed draft was rejected, probably because its proponent was not present, as well as because of its presumably strongly anti-Japanese tone. The text proposed by Sukarni and supported by the other *pemudas* present ran as follows:[68]

> "The Indonesian people hereby declares its independence. All existing governmental organs shall be seized by the people from the foreigners who still control them."

Hatta however objected: "As the youth say, only power can make the revolution successful. But power is not enough. The enemy, the true enemy is not Japan, who has been defeated in Indonesia, and has lost all power from now on. It is Holland that is trying to dominate Indonesia again." He saw no sense in a showdown with the Japanese at this stage.[69] After further heated discussion a final draft was produced, according to Malik and others by Sajuti Melik, according to Nishijima by the joint efforts of

---

66 Tan Malakka, *op. cit*, pp. 58f.
67 Nishijima, Kishi et al, *op. cit*., p. 500.
68 Cf. Sjahrir, *op. cit*., p. 258, and Malik, *op. cit*., p. 52.
69 Nishijima, Kishi et al., *loc. cit*.

Soekarno, Hatta, Subardjo, Maeda, Nishijima, Yashizumi and Miyoshi[70] This final draft was rather better adapted to the delicate position of the Japanese, and was generally less infammatory in tone. It read:[71]

> "We, the people of Indonesia hereby declare Indonesia's Independence. Matters concerning the transfer of power, and other matters, will be executed in an orderly manner and in the shortest possible time."

As Sjahrir commented bitterly, every word "that reflected our struggle against Japanese oppression and extortion disappeared from the draft of the Proclamation of the constitutional convention."[72]

A final dispute arose over who should have the honour of signing the Proclamation. Malik reports that the six (?) representatives of the *pemudas* wanted their names included without those of the older nationalists. But Soekarno adamantly rejected this idea. Finally, as a compromise, the Proclamation was signed by Soekarno and Hatta alone., The document was read solemnly aloud to the assembled representatives, who then mostly went home to bed. It was already 7:00 A.M., August 17th.[73]

It seems that the original plan agreed on for the public reading of the proclamation, was that it should take place on the Koningsplein (Ikada) in the presence of a hastily summoned but large crowd. Aidit reports that Suwirjo, the mayor of Djakarta, ordered his subordinate to make the necessary preparations. He adds however that the plans had to be changed because the *Kempeitai,* tapped the telephone lines, and so got wind of the scheme.[74] This may be the case. Another source however

---

70 Compare Malik, *loc. cit.*, with Nishijima, Kishi *et al.*, *loc. cit.*
71 Malik, *loc. cit.* Cf. also Hatta, "Isi Proklamasi" in *Fakta dan Doku-men2 untuk menjusun buku Indonesia memasuki Gelanggang Internasional'*, Supplemen I, Vol. XI, Kemlu R. I. Direktorat V, Seksi Pemjelidikan, Dokumentasi dan Perpustakaan (ed. Emzita), 1958, p. 1. He says that the second sentence of the Proclamation was geared to the question of how the instruments of power would pass from Japanese to Indonesian hands. "Matters concerning the transfer of power. in an orderly manner" meant that the Indonesians would attempt not to destroy their own forces in attempting to seize power. "....will be carried out.... in the shortest possible time," meant "before the Allies arrive."
72 Sjahrir, *op. cit.*, p. 258.
73 Malik, *op. cit.*, p. 52. Tan Malakka, *op. cit.*, p. 59, says the compromise suggestion was made by Chaerul Saleh, because the *pemudas* would not sign on the same paper with "Kempei nominees."
74 Probably the two readings were designed to satisfy two constituencies. The older leaders provided

affirms that Maeda, who had gone to bed before the actual signing of the Proclamation, and who up to this point had no idea of the 'Koningsplein proposal', found out about it when he woke up. Knowing that the Koningsplein would be stiff with Japanese tanks and guns protecting the radio-station and the *Kempeitai* headquarters situated on the square, he became very alarmed. It would take very little in such circumstances for the violence he had consistently tried to avoid, to break out. A nervous Japanese officer, or an overzealous Indonesian nationalist might spark a tragedy. He therefore contacted Subardjo, and impressed upon him the necessity of changing the plan.[75] Nishijima reports that on waking up that morning he too was startled to see out of the window "thousands of people of all ages and walks of life, marching in rows of four, like regular troops, towards the Koningsplein. They were carrying sharpened bamboo spears and red-and-white flags, and singing Indonesian songs." On telephoning to one of the Indonesian clerks at his office, he was told of a mass meeting to be held on the Koningsplein, where Soekarno would proclaim Indonesian Independence. Later however he heard that the site of the Declaration had been shifted to Soekarno's house on Pegangsaan near the Manggarai station.[76] This makes it look as if plans were changed only at the very last minute. The difficulty of Aidit's account is that it does not really explain how the fact of the *Kempeitai*'s knowing of the proposed meeting got back to the Indonesians (could it really have been through Maeda and Nishijima?), or how the change in plans was put into effect.

In any case it was not until 11:30 A.M. of the 17th that Soekarno, accompanied by Hatta, Abdul Latief, Dr. Muwardi and other dignitaries, read out the Proclamation in the courtyard of his own home at Pegangsaan 56.[77] The *Sang Merah Putih* was hoisted up a bamboo pole by Abdul Latief dressed in his Peta uniform, and *Indonesia Raya* was sung by all those present.

---

the Proclamation with P.P.K.I. endorse ment at Maeda's house. The *pemudas* had the satisfaction of an "open" proclamation among the "masses." Cf. Aidit, *op. cit.*, p. 509.
75 De Graaf, *op. cit.*, pp. 324f., quoting directly from Maeda.
76 Nishijima, *Verklaring.*, March 10-13, 1947, p. 8.
77 Kahin, *op. cit.*, p. 136. For a description of the scene by one of Soekarno's bodyguards, see R. O. Permadipura's article in*Pemandangan*, August 16, 1955. (By local Java time, the ceremony took place at 10:00 A.M.).

Though the Japanese military authorities kept a tight control over all the public presses in Djakarta, handbills announcing Independence were printed in the Naval Attache's office print-shop under Nishijima's supervision.[78] But it was not until 7:00 p. m. that evening that the Proclamation, together with Hatta's personal message to his old Nationalist comrades, was broadcast clandestinely from the Domei transmission-room.[79] The central radio station was still in the hands of the *Kempeitai*. General Nishimura's comment on this historic event was very much in character:[80]

> "About noon of this day, when I was in the office with the chief of the Planning Section and other personnel, my eyes caught a shabby sheet of paper brought in by a frightened and confused official, and all present there were suddenly taken aback, knowing that it was a propaganda sheet of Indonesian independence, and a part of the Indonesians had proclaimed independence breaking out of Japanese control."

But in Java, the reaction was great and growing enthusiasm. The Revolution had begun.

---

78 Nishijima, Kishi *et al, op. cit.*, p. 501.
79 Kahin, *loc. cit.*, and Hasjim Mahdan, *op. cit.*, The name of the man who succeeded in getting the broadcast was, according to Hasjim Mahdan, Sjachruddin.
80 *Statement* of Nishimura, April 10, 1947, p. 5. He adds that he then tried to collect the leaflets, find out where they were coming from, and suppress them, but was unsuccessful!

CHAPTER SEVEN
ALLIED STRATEGY AND THE PROBLEM OF EXPECTATIONS

Realities

On June 19, 1945 General MacArthur announed the transfer of the Netherlands East Indies from his own South-West Pacific Area Command to Lord Louis Mountbatten's South East Asia Command.[1] The transfer however only became of real significance after the Potsdam Conference. For it was only then that Mountbatten became aware of the existence of the Atom Bomb and the prospect of a speedy Japanese capitulation.[2] The political and military question of how Indonesia was to be approached and administered had however been the subject of dispute between American, Dutch and British officials for some time.[3] And it was only on August 24th that agreement was finally attained.[4] Under the terms of this agreement, the parties recognized that the re-occupation of the Netherlands East Indies would be a two-staged operation. In the first,

---

1 Cf., e. g. Brugmans,*etal*, *op. cit.*, p. 83. For the political manoeuvres between Dutch, American and British authorities at this time, see the excellent detailed analysis contained in Idrus Djajadiningrat, *The Beginnings of the Indonesian-Dutch Negotiations and the Hoge Veluwe Talks*, Cornell Modern Indonesia Project, Southeast Asia Program, Cornell University, Ithaca, N.Y., 1958, pp. 4-27.
2 F.S.V. Donnison, *British Military Administration in the Far East 1943-1946*, History of the Second World War Series, H. M, Stationary Office, London, 1956, p. 417.
3 Donnison, *op. cit.*, pp. 415f. For a text of the original van Mook-MacArthur understanding of December 10, 1944, and of the agreement of August 1945, cf. *Enquêtecommissie Regeringsbeleid 1940-1945, Militair Beleid, Terugkeer Naar Nederlandsch-Indie*, (8A en B), Staatsdrukkerijen Uitgeverijbedrijf, 's-Gravenhage, 1956, pp 632 634, 650-651.
4 The actual transfer of authority in the Netherlands-Indies from American to British hands was not made legally effective till August 15th, the day of the surrender. Cf. Rajendra Singh, *Post-War Occupation Forces: Japan and South-East Asia*, in the series *Official History of the Indian Armed Forces in the Second World War 1939-1945* (ed., Bisheshwar Prasad), Combined Inter-Services Historical Section, India and Pakistan, 1968, p. 220.

or military, stage, the South East Asia Command would have plenary powers to take any measures it might think fit to end the fighting in the islands. The Netherlands Indies Civil Affairs Administration (NICA) was in this early period to give unconditional obedience to the orders of the Supreme Commander. In return, the South East Asia Command would make no formal or public assumption of authority, and would see to it that the NICA was given as important a role as circumstances permitted.[5] Later, full powers would be handed over to the Dutch. Till then, however, the Allied Supreme Command would have complete jurisdiction over all personnel.

The changes in the South East Asia Command's jurisdiction should be understood for any just appreciation of the Allies' activities in the period under consideration. Half a million square miles were added to the million already under its jurisdiction. It acquired charge of an additional 80, 000, 000 people in addition to the 45, 000, 000 already assigned to it. And 2, 000 more miles were now included in an already grossly over — extended system of communications. It was therefore logical for the British to use the Japanese Army to keep control of the occupied areas, until they could arrive themselves. This meant that it was of the utmost importance to seize the nerve-centers of Japanese control in Southeast Asia, Saigon and Singapore, as soon as possible. Once these centers had been seized, the Allies could gradually take; over power in the conquered areas from the Japanese troops occupying them. In view of the importance of avoiding massive resistance on the part of the Japanese it was deemed advisable by MacArthur and Mountbatten to make no attempt to land forces in Malaya or Indonesia till after a formal surrender had been signed in Tokyo. The Dutch protested bitterly, since it was essential for their purposes that the Indonesians should not have the time to prepare a regime of their own, and they recognized that if the MacArthur-Mountbatten plan were followed,

---

5 Cf. *Aneta* (Manila) August 25, 1945 (as cited in U.S. Office of Strategic Services, Research and Analysis Branch, *Report #3250*, pp. 2f., September 1945) for the statement of General L. H. Van Oyen that "Once Batavia (Djakarta) is re-entered, the machinery for civil administration will be quickly re-introduced, and the Netherlands Indies Government, at present in Australia, will be likely to accompany the invasion forces or follow them shortly. For a time there will be a military administration in the Indies, but military control will be relinquished on the establishment of civil machinery."

Allied troops were unlikely to land on Java till late in September.⁶

Two other problems bedevilled the Allied strategists. The transfer of the Netherlands Indies to the South East Asia Command at such a late date meant Mountbatten had virtually no adequate basic intelligence on Indonesia, let alone any up-to-date information. The core of the Dutch intelligence service and civil administration had been concentrated at MacArthur's headquarters in Australia, which had been planned as the jumping-off point for an invasion of the Indies. There was no possibility, due to transport shortages, of shipping them *en masse* to Kandy, Rangoon or even Singapore. There was of course always the alternative, after August 17th, of recognizing and relying on the embryo Indonesian regime to maintain law and order on Java. But as we have seen, the British scarcely seem to have considered this at first. The demands of the Dutch and the logic of the re-conquest of Southeast Asia as a whole, inevitably cast the Japanese Army in the role of maintainer of the *status quo* in Indonesia. On Java, the full responsibility for carrying out this task was assigned to the Commander of the 16th Army.

The second difficulty was that of Allied ignorance of the political situation in Indonesia, especially on Java. Generally speaking there was little suspicion that the new Indonesian "regime" was anything but a Japanese puppet administration. Soekarno was certainly regarded as a quisling from his wartime broadcasts. Few believed he had any popular support whatever.⁷ This impression seems to have been sedulously fostered by "old Netherlands Indies hands." American intelligence apparently had a shrewder inkling of the real situation. An O.S.S. report dated August 13, 1945, commented:⁸

> "...(The Nationalist politicians) might conceivably consider the crucial period between actual Japanese surrender to the Allies,

---

6 See for details, Donnison, *op. cit.*, pp. 420ff., and Rajendra Singh, *op. cit.*, pp. 169f. Djakarta and Surabaja were fifth and sixth on the British list of Southeast Asian centres to be captured. Altogether 1 infantry division and 3 Air Force squadrons were initially assigned to accept the Japanese surrender on Java.
7 Cf. e. g. Donnison, *op. cit.*, pp. 422-425, and E. B. Van Hulten, *Rapport.*, July 24, 1946, p. 6. See also Kahin, *op. cit.*, p. 142, n. 8.
8 U.S. Office of Strategic Services, Research and Analysis Branch, *Report # 3229*, "Problems arising from a sudden liberation of the Netherlands East Indies," August 13, 1945, pp. 1f. These originally classified reports have recently been made available to scholars.

and the firm re-establishment of the Netherlands East Indies administration as their only precious chance to gain a strong bargaining position in relation to the government... A possibility therefore would be the formation... of an independent Indonesian government, which would disassociate itself from the Japanese and denounce them, or, if at all possible, revolt against them. This move would offer a chance of clearing the leadership group from the stigma of Japanese collaboration and create a purely Indonesian-Netherlands issue."

The Report went on to suggest that the Dutch select a group of trustworthy-Indonesians, including some collaborators, and give them interim charge of administration in Indonesia. Otherwise there would be trouble — and the United States would inevitably be identified as pro-colonial by the local population!

This seems to have been an exception to the rule however. The British seem to have been misled by their experience in Burma to expect little resistance from "native" administrators, and indeed felt that there would be no need for a tough policy. As one British officer later commented, "In Burma and Malaya, everywhere we had been hailed as liberators. Why do the people here (in Indonesia) alone look upon us with animosity?"[9] There is reason to believe that at the topmost levels, the British Labour Government's ideological position discouraged any very whole-hearted co-operation with the NICA, which was staffed by men who were not usually politically associated with the new leftist Dutch government, but were old pre-war colonial administrators. Lord Mount-batten, whose political savoir-faire in handling the Burmese problem has been generally acclaimed, and who had a generally liberal and progressive outlook, expressed at once the new British attitude towards colonialism and a more traditional British tendency to inane language, when he said, "Our one idea is to get the Dutch and Indonesians to kiss and make friends and then pull out."[10]

From all this it is important to understand that while *speed* was

---

9   Quoted by Anonymous Japanese Office, *Beschouwingen.*, June 21-23, 1947, p. 36.
10 Cited in Geoffrey Sawer, "Allied Policy in Indonesia," *Austral-Asiatic Bulletin*, April, 1946, p. 14.

essential for the Dutch, on whose mental horizon Indonesia loomed very large, to MacArthur and Mountbatten, Indonesia was very much a secondary affair, not at all at the centre of their attention. While the Dutch, Japanese and Indonesians might very well imagine that the Allies kept a hard, beady eye on Indonesia at every moment, the reality was very different. Power lay in the hands of the British and Americans, and naturally British and American interests were going to be seen to before the Dutch were allowed effectively to stake their claims.

Such was the rather confusing reality of the Allied approach to Indonesia. However two factors tended to distort the conception of this reality held by Indonesians and Japanese on Java. One was the nature of Allied communications to the islands. The other was the hopes and fears of their audiences.

Allied propaganda to Indonesia during the war seems to have centred around two main themes: 1) retribution for collaboration with the Japanese. 2) the promise of a new political relationship between Holland and her colony after the war was over. Most sources agree that Allied threats to punish severely those who gave aid and comfort to the enemy were important in creating an atmosphere of anxiety and uncertainty among the Indonesians. It was very easy, especially for those who feared that they might be affected, to see retribution as being the main Allied objective, whereas in reality of course it was very far down on their list of priorities.[11] Part of the weakness of the first post-Proclamation cabinet, was, as we shall see, this cloud which hung over the greater part of its membership.

Secondly, in spite of the ringing declaration of the Atlantic Charter and Allied propaganda about the San Francisco Conference, Dutch policy statements about Indonesia's future were made ambiguous by their great diversity. On December 12th, 1942, Queen Wilhelmina had made a speech in London, in which she announced the post-war creation of a Commonwealth "in which the Netherlands, Indonesia,

---

11 The Anonymous Japanese Officer, in his *Beschouwingen.*, p. 18, reports on the chilling effect of the broadcasts of Col. Abdul Kadir (later advisor to Van Mook) from Papua and Australia. The Colonel's repeated threat was that "When we go back to Java, we shall never forgive those who cried '*Amerika strika, Inggeris linggis!*' (Flatten America, use a crowbar on Britain!)." For some Indonesian reactions to these threats, see *ibid*, pp. 17-18.

Surinam and Curacao will participate with complete self-reliance and freedom of conduct in internal matters, but with readiness to render mutual assistance." Though she made no explicit promise that Indonesia would be allowed a free choice of government, she asserted that there would be "no room for discrimination according to race or nationality." The new relationship would be "a combination of independence and collaboration."[12] The then Foreign Minister of the Netherlands, van Kleffens, argued against immediate and full independence, preferring "progressive emancipation."[13] In June 1945, Professor Schermerhorn's new Government talked vaguely of "the liberation" of the "East Indies" from "Japanese oppression" as having "the utmost priority in all our endeavours."[14] In Australia, the acting Governor-General Hubertus van Mook, spoke of "the formation of a new state" based on "co-operation between Dutch and Indonesians."[15] The Dutch had also attempted to be tactful by changing their Ministry of Colonies into a Ministry for Overseas Territories; some radio-announcers even went so far as to speak of "Indonesians" instead of "natives." In July, 1945, the Minister for Overseas Territories, Logemann, made an unusually specific and liberal statement of Dutch intentions:[16]

> "The Netherlands is not going to reconquer a colony. It is going out for the liberation of the people of Indonesia... which it wishes to receive as a partner in the Kingdom of Queen Wilhelmina... After the war of steel, a spiritual struggle awaits us. The new responsibility which we assume in regard to the independence of Indonesia is not a mere formal action, let us say a democratic constitution on paper... Our Sovereign, as well as our Government and our people are ready to have the Netherlands fight only for an independent Indonesia and not for the restoration of the

---

12 For a text of the Queen's speech, see e. g. *Fakta dan Dokumen2*, pp. 218-220.
13 Cf. U.S. Office of Strategic Services, Research and Analysis Branch, *Report # 28769*, "Dutch Attitudes towards the Future of the Nether-lands East Indies," February 2, 1945, p. 1.
14 Quoted in *F.B.I.S. Reports*, June 29, 1945, section H, pp. 8f.
15 Quoted in *ibid.*, June 26, 1945, section Q, pp. 3f.
16 Speech of July 17, 1945, as quoted in U.S. Office of Strategic Services, Research and Analysis Branch, *Report # 3215*, July 23, 1945, p. 1. The Report is entitled, "New Netherlands Minister of Overseas Territories states Netherlands' Objectives in the Liberation of Indonesia."

colonial administration... We have the expressed demand of our democratic people that it does not want to fight for capitalistic and imperialistic objectives."

The liberality of Logemann was balanced by Major-General van Klemens, who can hardly have relieved many Indonesian minds by declaring that 100, 000 Dutch troops were ready to invade the Netherlands East Indies, and that he was sure the "natives... would be loyal, and co-operate fully with the Allies."[17] And General van Oyen announced that in his view all but a few dissidents would welcome the return of the Dutch. Trials would be held, but they would probably be few in number. He had the impression that the Japanese Occupation had left only one-tenth of one percent of the population influenced by Japanese propaganda.[18]

It is probable, however, that such varied and confusing statements were often taken by the Indonesians less as indication of doubt and conflict among Dutch policy-makers than as further examples of Dutch duplicity. The decision taken by the Allies to use the Japanese *enemy* rather than the "oppressed" Indonesians to maintain law and order, must surely at the start have undermined any possible Indonesian trust in Dutch intentions, and focussed Indonesian attention on the inescapable fact that the Dutch, not the Japanese, were their real antagonists.

Illusions, Plans, Stratagems:

a) The Japanese

Most accounts of the reactions and the "plans" of the Japanese in Indonesia at this time, tend to portray the Japanese as "Indonesia-centred" in their outlook. Yet a real understanding of Japanese behaviour, even at the higher levels, will be vitiated by such a perspective. The ordinary Japanese soldiers and middle-rank officers, who were unlikely to be affected by Allied war-crimes tribunals were far from being preoccupied with Indonesia's fate.

---

17 Quoted in *F.B.I.S. Reports*, June 24, 1945, section Q, p. 3.
18 See U.S. Office of Strategic Services, Research and Analysis Branch, *Report # 3250*, "Pre-Liberation Developments in the Netherlands East Indies," September 1945, citing an *Aneta* (Manila) bulletin of August 25, 1945.

From various Japanese reports one gets an impression of bewilderment, confusion and despair when the Imperial Rescript announcing the Emperor's surrender to the Allies was known.[19] Wild rumours of Allied revenge and the destruction of the homeland swept through the Army on Java. Even so cool and rational an observer as Nishijima notes parenthetically his own depression and feeling of desperation.[20] The majority of Japanese were concerned with just three things: getting safely out of Indonesia as rapidly as possible, seeing their homes and families, and doing what little they could to salvage something from the wreckage in Japan. Among the officer-corps this meant a hope that the position of the Emperor would somehow be maintained, and that Japan herself would not be razed by the invading barbarians. Psychological reactions to the collapse of the myth-system on which an entire generation had been reared varied from suicide, through complete apathy to 'last flings', orgies, etc.[21] Trained elite groups like the *Kempeitai* might carry on their work efficiently, but the majority of Japanese were morally shattered, and full of doubt and anxieties. Insofar as the Indonesians were involved in ordinary Japanese thinking, it was probably only tangentially. What attitude towards the Indonesians would allow them to get home as quickly and peacefully as possible?

At the higher levels of the Japanese Command of course, there were more complex issues at stake. General Yamamoto[22] and General Nishimura had been specifically instructed by the Allies to maintain order on Java. Their instructions ran:[23]

> a. Japanese commanders will be held responsible for ensuring that orders issued to them 1) are transmitted forthwith as

---

19 Cf. e. g. General Yamamoto, *General Report for Allied Headquarters from the 16th Army*, September 15, 1945, pp. 1f. ; *Statement* of Major Tadakazu Ishizima, November 16, 1946, p. 4; Nishijima, *Verklaring verbonden aan de politieke Afdeeling van het Marine -Kantoor te Batavia van Schoutbij Nacht Maeda*, March 25-29, 1947, p. 2. (Henceforth referred to as Nishijima, *Verklaring (Marine-Kantoor)*).
20 Nishijima, *Verklaring (Marine-Kantoor)*, March 10-13, p 8.
21 See e. g. Goro Taniguchi, "Indonesia to tomo ni ikite," (Having Lived with Indonesia), Volume 6 in *Hiroku Dai-Toa Sen Shi* (Secret History of the War for Greater East Asia), Fuji Shoen, Tokyo, 1954, pp. 534-539, translated by Y. Sasaki (*mimeo*).
22 He was acting for the *Saikosikikan*, General Nagano, who was then in Singapore.
23 From "*Orders for Japanese Surrender*," issued by HQ Allied Land Forces, South East Asia Command, August 18, 1945.

requisite to all troops under their command. 2) are implicitly obeyed.
b. Japanese commanders at all levels will be informed that pending further orders, they will be responsible for the maintenance of discipline among their own troops.
c. Japanese commanders will... be held responsible for the maintenance of public order... and the care and feeding of the civilian population.
d. Japanese commanders will be held responsible for the maintenance of all essential services.

Both generals could well expect to be held personally accountable at a Military Tribunal if they failed to carry out their task. This "responsibility" coincided with the natural inclinations of the two men, who seem to have been intelligent, strongly nationalist, and politically moderate officers. The Allies were expected to land at any moment. Any real aid they might give the Indonesians would only endanger their own lives, and perhaps even their country. Neither of the men can have doubted that the Allies, who had crushed Japan, would have any trouble or hesitation in stamping out a Republican Government.[24] Though neither of them seems to have been at all opposed on principle to Indonesian independence, Army ideology hardly encouraged them to stake their all on the aspirations of an alien people. Their first duty was to their homeland and Emperor. It was more than likely that "trouble" in Java would only harden Allied attitudes towards Japan and the Imperial family. A graphic, if not word for word report of a conversation between Nishimura and Maeda at this time, brings out these considerations clearly. Maeda had come to protest the Army's "reactionary" policy towards Indonesian Independence. Nishimura reportedly replied:[25]

> "We could help the Indonesians during war-time. But not now. Politically and strategically, Indonesian Independence is just another form of fighting. It makes no sense to stop fighting the

---

24 Cf. the Anonymous Japanese Officer, *Beschouwingen.*, June 21-23, 1947, p. 17.
25 *Ibid.*, p. 21.

Allies, but to urge on the Nationalists at the same time. The Emperor's will is not always the same. He ordered us to fight and we fought. Now he orders us to stop. We do not know the reason. But we should obey... Have you thought of the possible punishment the international world will inflict for such a breach of the capitulation agreement? It is easy to die. That is what we came here to do. But who is really going to suffer? Tokyo, the Government and the Emperor. Potsdam allowed the Emperor to stay on the throne... but will this promise be maintained if we break faith here?"

Major Ishizima, who was at Saigon during this period, reports a constant flow of telegraph messages from Java demanding instructions as to the proper course to be taken vis-à-vis Indonesian nationalist pressure: the answer was always that the 16th Army should try to maintain the *status quo*.[26]

The 16th Army generally gambled on a rapid landing of the Allies in considerable force. On this assumption, two basic tasks confronted them. One was maintaining discipline among their own men, the second was maintaining it among the Indonesians. As one observer put it, "Whether soldier or civilian, the Japanese were becoming desperate, nihilistic and idle, and military administration went into disorder."[27] Desertions were likely to break out, the authority of the officer-corps would be weakened, energy to carry out Allied commands would be hard to muster, and morale would be very low. As far as the Indonesians were concerned, three steps had to be taken immediately. All armed units would have to be disarmed and demobilized. Authority over Indonesian bureaucrats who how manned all but the very highest administrative posts had to be preserved. And a tight rein would have to be kept on *pemuda* activities. We shall see later how successful the Army was in carrying out these tasks.

Admiral Maeda and his group however seem to have been gambling on different assumptions and with different ends in mind, Nishijima, his right hand man at this period, notes that Maeda felt genuine sympathy with

---

26 *Statement* of Major Tadakazu Ishizima, November 16, 1946, p. 4.
27 Taniguchi, *op. cit.*, p. 534.

the Nationalist cause, and was not hampered by any official responsibility towards the Allies[28] And though, according to Major Ishizima, he had received explicit instructions from the Naval General Staff to keep out of the Indonesian Independence Movement, he does not seem ever to have taken these instructions very seriously.[29] He had no troops under his command; most of his aides were civilians. He had a far freer hand than his opposite number in the Army. He also seems to have had a keener appreciation of the 'emotional climate' on Java, and of the psychological consequences of the Proclamation he had done so much to put into effect.[30]

Maeda was basically concerned to do everything he could to unite the Nationalist leaders of all ages and groups, and to help prepare the Indonesians for a successful resistance to the re-imposition of Dutch colonial control. It is not certain quite what kind of "success" he envisaged, As has been suggested before, he seems to have tried to create a "candidate" echelon of leaders, primarily ex-graduates of the *Asrama Indonesia Merdeka*, to be led probably by the most notable of the "uncompromised" (in Allied eyes) nationalists — Tan Malakka or perhaps Sjahrir.[31] If, as seemed likely, Soekarno, Hatta and Subardjo were arrested, the struggle could be carried on by this reserve leadership. To strengthen Indonesia's hand, four steps had to be taken: 1) Armaments and ammunition had to be provided to the nationalists. 2) The Indonesians would need a group of trained personnel to help them in the operation (if necessary) of a guerilla resistance. 3) Any available Japanese funds would be most useful to a young Indonesian regime, at least until the Allies succeeded in cancelling the Japanese Military currency. 4) Avenues of communication between different parts of Java, between the various islands and on to the mainland would be extremely important.

There is reason to believe that Maeda and his colleague in Surabaja, Admiral Shibata, planned and succeeded in having large quantities

---

28 Nishijima, Kishi et al., *op. cit.*, pp. 473f. Also Nishijima, *Verklaring*, March 10-13, 1947, p. 9.
29 *Statement* of Major Tadakazu Ishizima, November 16, 1946, p. 4.
30 It is worth noting that Maeda had long connections with Indonesia going back to the pre-war period. He had also been a member of the Navy Ministry's Indonesian Policy Research Team. By contrast Nishimura came to Indonesia from China late in the occupation, and had developed no close ties with the Indonesian elite.
31 See Chapters I and III of this paper.

of arms, including even aeroplanes, moved out of Naval munitions dumps and arsenals. They were then turned over to certain Indonesians, particularly those of the younger generation, where they would be in 'safer' hands (i. e. less likely to be turned over willingly to the Allies. Claims have been made that a sizeable number of Japanese deserted before the Allies arrived and later went to work for the Revolution, bringing with them considerable quantities of packaged Japanese currency notes. It has also been alleged that Maeda was active in creating an inter-island network of small boats and fishing-smacks that could be used to carry information, guns, food and other necessities in an unobtrusive way, wherever they were needed.[32] There also were hints that in co-operation with certain Chinese businessmen, the groundwork was laid for extensive smuggling operations to mainland Southeast Asia.[33] It is difficult to estimate how true these allegations are. Many of them were made by Dutchmen in the years 1946-1947 when Holland had every interest in blackening the Republican cause by depicting it as Japanese-sponsored. But what one knows of the psychology and objectives of the Admiral and his friends does not lead one to suppose that the six weeks before the Allies arrived in Tandjung Priok harbour were spent in idle meditation. It is almost certain that a good part of the stories have a solid foundation in fact. The one remaining question about Maeda's attitude is whether, as some claim, he really anticipated Indonesian Independence alone, or looked forward to a period of turmoil in which the Allies would be unable to consolidate

---

32 Cf. Anonymous Japanese Officer, *Beschouwingen.*, June 21-23, 1947, pp. 7-9, 20-21, 25, 31-32, 38. He claims that the Republic thus started off with assets of 800, 000, 000 guilders of Japanese money, which even divided by 10 to allow for inflationary depreciation, was a considerable sum. He also puts the number of pro-Indonesian desertions at 7, 000. The same source lists Djakarta, Bogor, Bandung, Jogja (Naval aerodrome), Semarang, Madiun (Largest Naval aerodrome), Malang and especially the Surabaja naval base as the centres for Naval distribution of arms and ammunition to the Indonesians. In the last case, the transfer of armaments may have created the basis for the Battle of Surabaja in November, Cf. E. B. Van Hulten, *Rapport.*, July 24, 1946, pp. 4-6.

33 *Statement* of Captain Mizuta, March 14, 1946, p. 5. Cf. also E. B. Van Hulten, *Rapport.* July 24, 1946, p. 5, for a statement that Maeda, with the help of Yoshizumi and Mr. Maramis, created the organizational basis of the K.R.I.S., the famous Republican armed **unit formed mainly** from Christian Minahassans. Nishijima, in his *Verklaring (Marine-Kantoor)*, March 25-29, 1947, p. 2, ob serves that the Japanese faced the task of guarding 61 ammunition and oil dumps, 41 food storage warehouses, 44 internment camps, as well as power installations, water reservoirs, banks, business offices, etc., etc., scattered through 20 Residencies. The implication is that Japanese forces were spread too thin to be able to prevent large-scale looting and sabotage by groups of Indonesians. This may well be the case too; many Indonesian supplies were undoubtedly taken from the Japanese by violence, as well as through co-operation and diplomacy.

their power, after which the Japanese would be able to re-establish their supremacy in the area, having already established a bridgehead there during the occupation. Unfortunately, the question will probably remain unanswered for a long time to come.

b) The Indonesians

The expectations of the various groups of Indonesians in this period are difficult to unravel. At the risk of indulging in excessive speculation, the writer feels that roughly four separable 'opinion-groups' can be distinguished.

1) All observers testify to the fact that the Proclamation of Independence had an electrifying effect on the mass of Indonesians. The degree of excitation seems to have taken all parties by surprise, even those who claimed to be closest to the grass-roots. For example Adam Malik writes sadly, "The most regrettable thing was that the popular forces had had no real guidance before the Proclamation was made. The lack of any organization and leadership meant that the Revolutionary Army was like a flood, almost completely uncontrollable"[34] Suppressed hatred of the Japanese, exhilaration at the sight of their conquerors in defeat, and the elation of re-assuming control of their own destiny, produced reactions similar to those that had occurred after the Dutch collapse in 1941-1942, but many times more powerful. The reaction was of course not always purely political. Murder and looting were common in many areas. The Chinese, and those Dutchmen who had been released or escaped from Japanese concentration camps were in a particularly bad position. The Chinese, never very popular with ethnic Indonesians, had no military power to protect them from their enemies. Almost inevitably many tended to anticipate an Indonesian interregnum with alarm and hostility. Without necessarily being pro-Allied or pro-Dutch, they had good reason to be anti-Republican at this time, and to look forward to the imposition of firm Allied control in Indonesia as soon as possible. The Dutchmen who 'got loose,' seem in many cases to have found it hard to adjust to the new social and political situation, and tried to talk and act as they had

---

34 Malik, *op. cit.*, p. 59. Cf. also Maeda, *Beknopt Overzicht.*, September 26, 1945, pp. 2f.

done before 1942 — with results unpleasant but wholly predictable.[35]

These observations are not intended to discount the vast popular enthusiasm for independence, but rather to suggest that this enthusiasm was amorphous, without organized channels along which it could flow. As Dr. Hatta expressed it:[36]

> "Every revolution invariably gives rise to an atmosphere influenced by a mass psychology, which is itself strongly affected by romanticism and heroism. The primary problem in a revolution is how to channel the burning but anarchic energies of the masses, and to mould them into a body, strong at heart, capable of enduring suffering and undergoing trials in facing reactions that may arise, until the final victory is achieved.... For revolutions that break out suddenly and are sustained by burning enthusiasms are faced by reactions who possess co-ordinated control over the instruments of power."

In an impending revolutionary situation, the range of actions seen as "liberating" extend far beyond those usually considered 'political.' Independence, for the masses, was something unconnected with institutions, words, agreements, signatures, but rather a matter of *"semangat"* (spirit), symbols, voices, violent direct action, conquest, comradeship, destruction and spiritual solidarity. In the revolutionary universe, the distinction between *Rampok* (roughly 'looting') and confiscation, murder and revolutionary struggle, inevitably tended to be blurred. Fears and hopes assumed titanic proportions. It was a situation where only charismatic authority could have any controlling and guiding effect. We shall see the difficulties this was to give the established leadership.[37]

---

35 Cf. *Statement* of Captain Kiso Tsuchiya, April 3-8, 1947, p. 4. See also D. Wehl, *The Birth of Indonesia*, George Allen & Unwin, Ltd., London, 1948, generally for some sharp comments on the internment camps, guards and prisoners alike — though the author's point of view is definitely pro-Dutch.
36 Hatta, "Isi Proklamasi," in *Fakta dan Dokumen2 (Supplemen I)*, p. 1.
37 Cf. Prof. Dr. P. M. van Wulfften-Palthe, *Psychological Aspects of the Indonesian Problem*, E. J Brill, Leiden, 1949, pp. 27-32,45-50, for some interesting comments on the mood of the early revolution as seen through hostile Dutch eyes. The rest of the book is too partisan to be of much use.

2) This leadership, which centred in these early days around Soekarno, Hatta and perhaps Subardjo, was faced with a major political dilemma. It correctly entertained grave fears about Allied, and particularly Dutch, intentions. There was reason to believe that the Allies would regard them in a doubly unfavorable light — both as collaborators with the Japanese and as rebels against Dutch authority. The Japanese Army, increasingly concerned to maintain law and order (the *status quo*) for political and 'survival' reasons, and realizing that Soekarno and Hatta were dangerously powerful symbols to the mass of the population, would certainly be hostile to any obvious encouragement of a revolutionary upheaval. If the Allies wanted the two leaders tried for "collaboration," the Army was unlikely to worsen its position by permitting them to disappear.[38] Furthermore, though it was obvious that the Japanese had only physical force, and the threat of massive retaliation to maintain their position, and that therefore there was a good deal of leeway within which the Indonesians could operate politically without forcing a show-down, the fear of provoking the Japanese to violent repression was an important consideration in the established Indonesian leadership's thinking. However, on the other side, the pressure from the youth, the undergrounds and the masses to give positive signs of Independence, was steadily rising. If it was not given orderly means of satisfaction, the prestige of the top leadership and its political effectiveness threatened to be seriously undermined. Luckily however, the immediate demands of the period were less for 'practical' power than for the bold wielding of the symbols of authority. This perhaps explains why so much of the early struggle between Japanese and Indonesians centred around 'symbolic' actions such as raising the Indonesian flag on public buildings, holding mass rallies, and broadcasting revolutionary speeches.[39]

This meant that for a short time the established leadership did not have to try to withdraw power from the Japanese Army where it would have been most vitally felt — in the administration. They could — and

---

38 Cf. *Statement* of Captain Kiso Tsuchiya, April 3-8, 1947, pp. 8f. Nishijima, *Verklaring (Marine-Kantoor)*, March 25-29, 1947, pp. 2f. E. B. Van Hulten, *Rapport.*, July 24, 1946, p. 6.
39 See the letter of General Yamamoto to Admiral Patterson, dated September 23, 1945, where he warns the British particularly against interfering with such revolutionary and nationalist symbols. See also Kahin, *op. cit.*, p. 137.

had to — depend on a gradual osmotic process whereby the Indonesians in the bureaucracy could imperceptibly assume the psychological upper hand, and effectively take over practical control. But very soon effective control of the bureaucracy would be of overwhelming importance, not simply as a solid way of backing the international claims of the new regime, but also as a means of co-ordinating, centralizing and controlling *pemuda* anarchism, and preventing alternative groups from outflanking the top leadership by demands for concerted radical action against the Japanese.[40]

The established leadership was thus the focal point for conflicting pressures exerted by Indonesians, Japanese and — from a distance — the Allies. The one way of trying to resolve these conflicts was to establish an unobtrusive but effective and co-operative administration as soon as possible. Needless to say, this was easier planned than done. But such a policy promised to allow the *pemudas* to expend their energies usefully at the grass-roots level in administrative rather than agitational politics. If it should happen that the British (or the Americans) were the first Allied contingent to land, their partial support might be won by a show of competence and full co-operation. And if the Dutch arrived first, the bargaining position of the new regime would be strengthened proportionately to the effectiveness of its governmental authority. For the Dutch would certainly use any signs of lack of control as an excuse for hostile moves against the Republic. Finally, an *orderly* transition from 'symbol manipulation' to practical routine administration would do much to allay the personal fears of the Japanese, and avoid any violent intervention. In effect, the political objectives of the established leaders was to create a working administration, and to build up a position where

---

40 Hatta, in "Isi Proklamasi" (in *Fakta dan Dokumen2, SupplemenI*), p. 4 observes; "There was another way to power — the seizure of power from the Japanese by building up a national governmental administrative arm alongside the one controlled by the Japanese. This way might seem to be revolutionary — but not rational. *And what is not rational in a revolution is not revolutionary*. This second method would only have created difficulties and slowed down the transfer of power into our hands. It is very probable that it would have caused a violent struggle, and the victory would not certainly have been ours. It would have created two different government administrations side by side. As a result the new national administration, just set up, would not have been able to work effectively, while the administrative structure capable of working effectively would have been allowed to fall into the hands of the Japanese, to be then handed over to the Allies." The underlining is the writer's. One can imagine *pemuda* reaction to the underlined phrase.

the Allies might be willing to compromise with them to avoid trouble. But in the face of the enormous forces that had destroyed the Japanese Empire, and the highly delicate and precarious balance of power on Java which threatened to break down at any moment into violence and anarchy, the established leaders cannot have been too optimistic. The relative inconspicuousness of the first Cabinet may perhaps be attributed partly to its unwillingness to do anything to antagonize the powerful political forces that surrounded it.

The two remaining groups have much in common. In essence they were the circles around Sjahrir and Tan Malakka. 3) There is every reason to believe that Sjahrir, who spent much of the summer of 1945 listening to Allied radio broadcasts, developed a shrewd estimate of the probable situation in the immediate post-war period. In the face of dominant Anglo-Saxon power in the Southeast Asian area, Indonesia would probably need a leadership untainted by any suspicion of collaboration, unimpeachably Nationalist, and yet recognized as comparatively moderate and pro-Western. It can hardly have failed to occur to him, that with the possible exception of Amir Sjarifuddin, he himself was the one man who could fulfill these requirements.[41] In a less explicit way, much of the younger generation was to come to similar conclusions. Sjahrir was a member of the 'older generation,' but he provided a clear and 'respectable' focus for anti-leadership feelings which were strong at the time among the youth. For the younger generation was to become increasingly disturbed by the cautious tactics of their elders, and the obvious distaste and alarm their revolutionary activity caused among sections of the traditional *prijaji* and Moslem elites, who tended to look to the established nationalist leadership for protection against *pemuda* 'attentions.' The youth certainly felt borne up on a tide of popular revolutionary enthusiasm, and were in strong opposition to anything that smacked too much of "order," "discipline" and bureaucratic timidity. Much of their psychology was, as Maeda put it, frankly "anarchic," utterly opposed to the "diplomacy" of

---

41 In the event, his calculations were partially upset by the slow Allied advance, which allowed the flood of undisciplined revolutionary fervour to rise to a point where he alone could no longer control it. It must have been clear that Soekarno was an essential component of any Republican leadership from the moment that it became clear that he was the one man who to some degree could control it.

the older generation.[42]

4) Tan Malakka appears to have relied on the same kind of groups as Sjahrir, though he had different long-term objectives in mind. Whereas Sjahrir was in the long run hurt by the delayed Allied arrival in Indonesia, Tan Malakka was able to use the time to good effect. Some mystery surrounds his activities *before* the Proclamation. According to his own account he spent most of the Occupation working at a coal-mine at Bayeh in Banten, hiding from the Japanese authorities under an assumed name, However there is some reason to believe that the Japanese knew that he was on Java, and possibly even where he was. The Japanese Army seems to have believed him to be an important figure in Communist circles, and a number of fake Tan Malakkas were "produced" by them on several occasions in various parts of Java. For what purpose, is not quite clear, The most probable reason is that they hoped to lure members of the Com-munist Party into betraying themselves by trying to contact him. An alternative theory is that they were trying to test Tan Malakka's popularity in case he was needed to head the anti-Allied movement. But this seems a little far-fetched in view of the Army's general political outlook and level of sophistication. Another source indicates that he was seen talking to certain high Naval officers at the Banten coal mine just before the surrender[43] If this story is true, the "Naval officers" were presumably associates or assistants of Admiral Maeda's. Tan Malakka himself says, rather confusingly, that he was in contact with certain youth leaders from May 1945 onwards[44] and that he arrived in Djakarta on August 15th, and stayed at Sukarni's house, though concealing his identity from all, including even Sukarni![45] It is not impossible that he was covertly involved in the Rengasdengklok affair. One source at least avers that he spent his time at Sukarni's urging a coup d'état.[46] After the

---

42 Maeda, *Beknopt Overzicht.*, September 26, 1945, pp. 2-3. Incidentally, this short memorandum of Maeda to Admiral Patterson is an excellent political and psychological analysis of the period.

43 See Kahin, *op. cit*, pp. 118ff. Tan Malakka, *op. cit.*, p. 67, confirms, with some satisfaction, the stories about the false Tan Malakka's, which, he says, were used by the Japanese and Dutch(!) to confuse patriots. He adds that when he got to Bogor early in October, and met Sukarni and Adam Malik again, they gave him a very hard look-over. Apparently they had on several occasions nearly been trapped by the fake Tan Malakkas.

44 Tan Malakka, *op. cit.*, pp. 55f. For another aspect of his activities, see Chapter IV of this paper.

45 Tan Malakka, *op. cit.*, p. 55.

46 Cf. *Fakta dan Dokumen2*, p. 154. Sukarni was then living on Djalan Fort de Kock.

Proclamation he is reported to have gone to live with Nishijima, and from there contacted Admiral Maeda, in order to ask his advice as to what political strategy he should adopt. The Admiral seems to have counselled him to drop all "Communistic propaganda" in favour of Nationalism, and reminded him that the pre-war "Popular Front" line supporting bourgeois nationalism was still orthodox.

His activities for the rest of August and September are somewhat obscure, though he was in contact with Mr. Subardjo from August 25th on, according to his own account,[47] and probably much earlier. One story has it that the two men were preparing to dispense with Soekarno and Hatta, and possibly in temporary alliance with Sjahrir, assume national leadership.[48] It is probable that Tan Malakka was concerned in this period to build up an organization and a reputation independent of the Soekarno-Hatta leadership, so that he would be free to act on his own if and when a crisis arose. This strategy would mean staying temporarily in the background.[49] Whatever his ultimate purposes were, it is enough for our purposes to understand that the essential difference between Tan Malakka and Sjahrir lay in their attitude to the revolutionary surge that was beginning to sweep Java. Tan Malakka welcomed the growing anarchy and disorder, hoping that out of the confusion and excitement a more radical and tough-minded temper would emerge. This in turn would help to precipitate a struggle with either the Japanese or the Allies, And in such a struggle, his own peculiar talents for underground revolutionary organization and agitation would be shown to their best advantage. In contrast, Sjahrir feared and distrusted the anarchical, destructive side of the revolutionary movement as inevitably leading to a massive and violent Allied intervention and probably to deep internal conflict and bitterness in Indonesian society as well. It was probably his hope that a

---

47 Tan Malakka, *op cit.*, p. 61. They had also probably been in contact in Japan during the thirties. (See footnote 134 for a brief comparison of Maeda's and Tan Malakka's political outlook.) Tan Malakka recalls that he had not seen Subardjo since 1922 in Holland, and Subardjo thought he was dead. It was through Subardjo that he then met Iwa Kusumasumantri and Sajuti Melik, and later Soekarno, Hatta, Sjahrir, Mr. Gatot, and Dr. Buntaran.
48 For an extended and subtle account of Tan Malakka's and Subardjo's activities at this time, see Kahin, *op. cit.*, pp. 147-170.
49 There is however a story that Tan Malakka was offered any *new* position in the first Republican Cabinet that he cared to have. This would have allowed him to take the portfolios of either Foreign Affairs or Information. But not too surprisingly, he rejected the offer.

more regularized form of politics would emerge in which his intellectual and diplomatic talents would be most usefully employed. Indonesia's immediate interests would be best served, he may have felt, not on the barricades but at the conference table.

CHAPTER EIGHT
THE FINAL CONFLICT WITH THE JAPANESE AND THE BEGINNINGS OF A NEW REGIME

(From the Proclamation of Independence to the First British Landing on Java.)

As soon as Nishimura got word of the Proclamation he took steps to minimize any effects it might have. Orders from the Allies had already forbidden the Japanese to permit broadcasts of any kind anywhere. Nishimura used this as a pretext for continuing to bar the Indonesians from all radio-stations.[1] The distribution of nationalist posters and leaflets was forbidden.[2] Soekarno and Hatta were summoned to Nishimura's office to "explain themselves." According to one account, they told him that they had been forced to issue the declaration (presumably the 'public' declaration at Pegangsaan 56) by *pemuda* elements, but that anyway Japan had after all promised them independence. Nishimura replied that he could not permit the Indonesians to jeopardize Japan's position vis-a-vis the Allies, and therefore he would not yield to Indonesian persuasion, even though Soekarno guaranteed that no violent seizure of power would be attempted in Djakarta. At a meeting on the 19th with General Yamamoto, the two leaders received the same answer.[3]

---

1 *Statement* of Nishimura, April 25, 1947, p. 8. Not only were the radio-stations heavily guarded (one attack by Medical College students was fended off) but as an added precaution the vacuum tubes in the transmitters were removed.
2 Nishimura says that the *Kempeitai* was not called into the case "because we still felt that the leaflets were a gesture." See *Statement* of Nishimura, April 25, 1947, p. 8, and *Statement* of Nishimura, April 10, 1947, p. 5.
3 Cf. *Statement* of Nishimura, April 10, 1947, p. 6; *Statement* of Nishimura, April 25, 1947, pp. 8f. Nishijima, Kishi, *et al., op. cit.*, pp. 509f. Cf. A.M. Hoeta Soehoet, *op. cit.*, in D. Marpaung, ed., *op. cit.*, p. 34.

The first move on the Republican side therefore was to call an 'unauthorized' session of the P.P.K.I. on the morning of August 18th. Soekarno nominated 6 new members to the Committee.[4] The meeting was also attended by three Japanese, Nishijima, Miyoshi and Saito, all of whom had been at Maeda's house the night the Proclamation had been drafted and signed.[5] Nishimura testifies to the equivocal policy of the Japanese Army, which presumably felt that a sedate meeting of the P.P.K.I. was better than revolutionary agitation among the Indonesian masses. He notes that Yamamoto sent word via certain Japanese members (of the P.P.K.I.) denouncing the meeting (but doing nothing to break it up). Moreover, the denunciatory note was not delivered until the 19th. On August 18th, Yamamoto did nevertheless summon the members of the P. P. K. I, to outline the official position of his administration on the question of independence. He told them that:[6]

"Japan has accepted the Potsdam Declaration, and accordingly assistance towards Independence is impossible; the military administration on Java will be continued under the command of the Supreme Commander-in-Chief of the Japanese Army, in conformity with the principles of maintaining the *status quo*, while firmly securing peace and good order, until the day when the transfer of everything to the Allies is completed."

When the newly enlarged P.P.K.I. met on the morning of the 18th, its first task was the consideration of the draft Constitution bequeathed to it by the B.P.K.I. The bulk of the draft was in fact approved, though a number of significant modifications were accepted. Of these the most important were:

---

4 These six members cause some difficulties. Pringgodigdo, in *Perubahan Kabinet Presidensil Mendjadi Kabinet Parlementer*, p. 16, and Yamin, ed., *op. cit.*, pp. 399 473, name Subardjo, Kasman Singodimedjo, R.A.A. Wiranatakusuma, Sajuti Melik, Iwa Kusuma-sumantri and Ki Hadjar Dewantoro. Malik, *op. cit.*, p. 61, and Nishijima, Kishi, *et al.*, *op. cit.*, p. 512, however, name Sukarni, Wikana and Chaerul Saleh rather than Sajuti Melik, Iwa Kusumasum-antri and Ki Hadjar Dewantoro. The solution may be that Pringgodigdo and Yamin's three members were installed when the three youth leaders walked out of the meeting (for which see below).
5 See e. g. Tan Malakka, *op. cit.*, p. 60.
6 *Statement* of Nishimura, April 10, 1947, p. 5.

1. The elimination of large parts of the Preamble, particularly the more fulsome references to Japan.
2. The removal, on Hatta's initiative, of the stipulation that the President would have to be a Moslem. Hatta observed that the provision was needlessly offensive to religious minorities, and that since *in fact* the President was bound to be a Moslem, deletion of the provision would unite all groups in full support of the Constitution.[7]
3. The deletion, again at Hatta's urging, of the controversial phrase binding Moslems to the performance ot their religious duties as a matter of constitutional law.
4. A declaration of qua si-constitutional status by Dr. Supomo, guaranteeing the institution of provincial autonomy, though no such guarantee was included in the Constitution itself.[8]
5. Two supplementary regulations, added as a sort of appendix to the Constitution, giving the President near-dictatorial emergency powers for an initial six-month period.[9]
6. A group of transitional regulations for the election of the President and Vice-President by the P.P.K.I., confirming the interim powers of the P.P.K.I. and declaring that all previous laws not specifically repealed would continue in effect. One of these regulations stipulated that until the D.P.R. and the M.P.R. were formed, their functions would be fulfilled by the President with the assistance of a National Committee. Some difficulty arose here because a group of members wanted the P.P.K.I. as a whole to choose the membership of the National Committee, whereas others felt that the President should have full discretion. Eventually the group

---

[7] Thus at one blow Soekarno's concession to Moslem sentiment at the last meeting of the B.P.K.I. was gone. It was an indication of the now completely subordinate role the religious leaders were playing that not a voice was raised in real protest.

[8] Dr. Ratulangie strongly criticized the draft Constitution, saying that "the administrative areas in the various larger islands should be given the broadest possible right to see to their own needs as they see fit themselves. of course with the understanding and agreement that these areas are areas of Indonesia, of one state. but the needs of the areas must be heeded, i. e. by establishing some regulation which will hand over to the provincial government full powers to order their own regional affairs." Yamin, ed., *op. cit.*, p. 412.

[9] The key provision read: "During the space of six months after the end of the Greater East Asian War, the President of Indonesia shall order and regulate all matters laid down in this Constitution." See e.,g. Yamin, ed., *op. cit.*, p. 34.

favoring Presidential initiative won, upon Hatta's assurance that full representation of all Indonesian groups would not be impaired under this arrangement.[10]

Although the bulk of the Committee's work that morning was conducted in a sedate and business-like fashion, as described above, one rather unpleasant scene did take place, at least according to Malik and Tan Malakka. As the meeting was about to begin, Chaerul Saleh launched into a fierce attack on the legitimacy of the P.P.K.I. itself, a body which he said "stank" of the Japanese, Now that independence had been proclaimed, he said, all chains that bound them to such creations of the Japanese were broken. He demanded that the meeting be moved to a public place, where the masses could take part, and insisted that the committee be called the *Komite Nasional Indonesia* and no longer the P.P.K.I. Malik, supported by Tan Malakka, goes on to say that in reply. "Hatta explained that for himself and Soekarno it was difficult to separate their *responsibility* to the Japanese from their *duty* to the people. For this reason, said Hatta... we tell the Japanese that this is a meeting of the P.P.K.I., while we guarantee to the people that this is a meeting of the *Komite Nasional Indonesia Pertama*." When asked by Hatta, Soekarno nodded his head in assent. Angered by what Malik venomously calls Hatta's "hermaphroditic" statement, Chaerul Saleh, Sukarni and Wikana then supposedly stalked out of the meeting.[11]

Whether the story is true or not is essentially unimportant. Its contours reveal clearly enough what Hatta called the "legalism" of the youth, but which is perhaps more precisely described as a deep need for strong "symbolic action." Both sides recognized the undesirable features of the P.P.K.I., but Hatta, a man involved in real consideration of practical power, attached much less significance than the youth to the Committee's

---

10 Yamin, ed., *op. cit.*, pp. 428-431.
11 Malik, *op. cit.*, p. 61. (Italics are Malik's) Cf. Tan Malakka, *op. cit.*, p. 60. Tan Malakka says that Chaerul Saleh, Wikana, Sukarni *and Adam Malik* were invited to attend the meeting by Soekarno. After consultations with *pemuda* groups centred at Kramat (near the Medical School) they agreed to go. When they arrived however and found three Japanese there, they boycotted the meeting at once. In the meantime they had also envisaged a "planning committee" to lay down national goals, to be called the Indonesian National Committee. Soekarno and Hatta would be obliged to carry out this Committee's plans. A popular military arm was to be set up under a *Kommissie van Aksie* (Action Committee). See also Nishijima, Kishi, *et al.*, *op. cit.*, pp. 413f.

symbolic status. By their actions, the youth were able to wash their hands of the cautious compromises that the Committee was trying to hammer out. Probably the departure of the youth representatives contented both groups in different ways.

Left to themselves, the 'older' leadership continued their discussions until 3:15 p. m., when Soekarno announced that the press outside was eagerly awaiting the news of the election of Indonesia's first President. The nomination of Soekarno as President and Hatta as Vice-President by Oto Iskandardinata was greeted with acclamation, and amid cheers and the singing of *Indonesia Raya*, the two leaders were formally elected. The Executive, with its temporary "absolute powers" and the Constitution were now officially established.[12]

On August 19th, the P.P.K.I. met again. After much technical discussion of jurisdictions, names, titles and offices for regional administration, general agreement was reached on the division of Indonesia into 8 provinces, each with three levels of local government. These would be: at the Provincial level a Governor and a National Regional Committee, at the Residency level a Resident with a National Residency Committee, and at the village level a *kepala desa* with a village council. Special provisions were laid down for municipalities, but along the lines of former Dutch practice. The status of the Princely States was left deliberately vague. Teukoe Hasan, Pangeran Mohammad Noer, Dr. Ratulangie, Mr. Latuharhary and Pudja were designated the first Governors of Sumatra, Kalimantan, Sulawesi, Maluku, and the Lesser Sundas respectively. A series of important basic regulations for centralizing the police force, controlling the distribution of medical supplies, regrouping assorted military units into a national army, liberalizing regional autarchy, collecting reserves of food and clothing and controlling their prices, establishing a legal currency, setting up a Central Government Office, with its own Information Bureau, co-ordinating all communications, purging the bureaucracy and the police of undesirable elements-all were approved. There was particular enthusiasm for a general political amnesty.[13]

---

12 Yamin, ed., *op. cit*. pp. 425-427. Cf., however, Tan Malakka, *op. cit*., p. 60. He comments sourly that Soekarno and Hatta were elected quite undemocratically, without any opposition, and on the express instructions of Marshal Terauchi (!)
13 Yamin, ed., *op. cit*., pp. 438-452. The amnesty read: "We hereby proclaim that we, the President of

A Committee consisting of Subardjo, Sutardjo and Kasman Singodimedjo outlined a plan for the future ministries of the new government. Much of the discussion was technical, and concerned the most efficient distribution of functions and jurisdictions. However two interesting political proposals were also made. A projected Ministry of Religious Affairs was subjected to violent attack by Mr. Latuharhary (a Christian), as bound to cause discontent whether it was run by Moslems or Christians. Partly as a result of his vehemence the proposed Ministry was voted down 6 to 19.[14] Secondly Dr. Amir suggested the creation of a Department for Youth Affairs "to enable us as soon as possible to start militarizing and training the ideology of our youth." This idea was given partial support by Iwa Kusumasumantri who in his turn urged the creation of a *Staatspartij* (State Party) under the Ministry of Information. He said it would be "a party to support the government... to build up our new country."[15] These suggestions were voted down for the time being. But as we shall see, the idea of a national party, at least, remained very much alive.

Twelve ministries having been decided upon, the problems of local administration were next considered. Debate centred on how to get instructions flowing out to the local National Committees, how to build up a strong political organization to harness the energies of the masses and how to compel the Japanese to surrender their offices to Indonesians at a more rapid rate. Eventually however the Committee decided that in view of the delicate political situation these were problems best left to the President's discretion. He would be more likely to persuade the Japanese not to be obstructive. More could perhaps be accomplished in private conversations and private understandings than by resolutions and slogans. President Soekarno wound up the meeting by agreeing that these were matters that might well be left discreetly vague till power was handed over. He promised to try to persuade the military authorities to be as co-operative as possible.[16] Although there had been a general wish among the Committee members to name specific people to the Ministries

---

Indonesia, will immediately take advantage of our privilege to free those who are held punishable on political grounds. For this purpose a careful investigation will be set up."

14 Yamin, ed., *op. cit.*, pp. 457, 462.
15 Yamin, ed., *op, cit.*, pp. 457, 458, 460.
16 Cf. Yamin, ed., *op. cit.*, pp, 453-473, and especially pp. 472-473.

newly established by the P.P.K.I., no such step was taken at that time. The Japanese were extremely hostile to any such idea. It seemed to them that the Allies would never tolerate such open complaisance towards the new regime.[17]

Meeting again on August 22nd, the P.P.K.I. made two further important decisions. The first was to make further arrangements for the establishment of the Komite Nasional Indonesia Pusat (K.N.I.P. — Central Indonesian National Committee) the formation of which had apparently been somewhat delayed by the differences of opinion revealed in the meeting on August 18th concerning the role which the P.P.K.I. itself would have in setting up the body which was destined to replace it.[18] Shortly afterwards Soekarno and Hatta appointed 135 members from a large number of different ethnic, political and other groupings, including all the members of the P.P.K.I. except themselves, to the new body.[19] On August 29th, President Soekarno dissolved the P.P.K.I. and inaugurated the K.N.I.P. which, according to Section 4 of the Constitution's Transitional Regulations, was to act as an advisory body to the President and his Cabinet.[20] In the next few months the new body steadily gained in power. In addition to this civilian 'directorate', a skeleton military organization was adumbrated (for which see below), to be known as the *Badan Keamanan Rakjat* or B.K.R.[21] Secondly the P.P.K.I. reversed

---

17 Pringgodigdo, *Perubahan Kabinet Presidensil Mendjadi Kabinet Parlementer*, pp. 20-21.
18 For indications of further complications surrounding the question of the formation of the K.N.I.P. see Hatta's oblique references in the discussions of August 18th to a "Komite Nasional" already in existence, of which the P.P.K.I. was "only a part" (Yamin, ed., *op. cit.*, pp. 428-430), and Tan Malakka's mention of *pemuda* plans to set up their own National Committee (note 327 above). The terms "Kornite Nasional" (used in the Constitution), "Komite Nasional Indonesia," "Komite Nasional Pusat" and "Komite Nasional Indonesia Pusat" were used almost interchangeably in these early days. For the text of the P.P.K.I. 's August 18th announcement on the formation of the K.N.I.P. see *Asia Raya*, August 25, 1945, and Koesnodi-prodjo, ed., *Himpunan Undang2, Peraturan2, Penetapan2, Pemer-intah Republik Indonesia, 1945*, new revised edition, Djakarta, 1951, p. 117.
19 On these appointments see Kahin, *op. cit.*, pp. 139f.
20 The provision reads: "Prior to the formation of the People's Deliberative Assembly, the People's Representative Council Parliament, and the Supreme Advisory Council according to this Constitution, all their powers shall be exercised by the President with the assistance of a National Committee." Yamin, ed., *op. cit.*, p. 34.
21 Koesnodiprodjo, *Himpunan. 1945*, pp. 118-120. The B.K.R. was formally a section of the *Badan Penolong Keluarga Korban Perang* (B.P.K.K.P. — Organization for Aid to the Families of Victims of War), which was established at the same time. The B.P.K.K.P. was a continuation of the Japanese-sponsored B. P. P. (*Badan Pembantu Pradjurit*, later *Badan Pembantu Pembelaan*) which gave assistance to Peta members and their families. Oto Iskandardinata, the head of the former B. P. P.,

its previous attitude towards Iwa Kusumasumantri's proposal for a State Party. It agreed that a single national party, the *Partai Nasional Indonesia* (Indonesian National Party), should be formed, to include all groups. Soekarno said of this party that it would become "the 'motor' of the people's struggle in every sphere and in every field." He added that "the National Committee is a committee, the Indonesian National Party is a party. The Committee is set up for a temporary period, the party we need also to continue into the future." Its tasks would be: "to strengthen the unity of the Nation and State, to increase the feelings of love, loyalty and service to the native land; to make efforts to work out the economic and social program as mentioned in the Constitution of the Republic of Indonesia; to assist in the achievement of social justice and of the principle of humanity by means of international peace."[22] On August 27th, the top leadership of the new party was announced as including Sajuti Melik, Iwa Kusumasumantri, Sudjono, Wikana, Maramis, and various other associates of President Soekarno and Mr. Subardjo.[23] The basis for the party was to be the structure of the old *Djawa Hookookai*, though the names, for example, of the local units would be changed. Initially at any rate, the new party was to inherit the membership of its predecessor.[24] It was hoped that in this way the party would be able to mobilize mass support for the regime at the grass-roots level without too much difficulty. It would also provide the leadership with an institutional support more flexible and dynamic than the administrative bureaucracy. However the P.N.I. stayed in existence for scarcely a week. On August 31st, it was suddenly dissolved.[25] The reasons for its early demise may include the fact that its top leadership largely coincided with the membership of the P.P.K.I. — K.N.I.P. It may also be true that its leaders bowed to a general feeling that a "State Party" was unlikely to be very popular with the Allies

---

continued as head of the B.P.K.K.P.
22 Radio speech by President Soekarno, August 23, 1945, entitled, "The Change of the Times and Our Duty," cited in *Fakta dan Dokurnen2*, pp. 4-10. For the announcement of the P.P.K.I. decision establishing the P.N.I. see Koesnodiprodjo, *Himpunan. 1945*, p. 118.
23 *Asia Raya*, August 28, 1945.
24 Generally speaking, the old *Djawa Hookookai* leadership seems gradually to have been ousted by younger, more revolutionary elements. At the same time, the units of the organization, failing to become parts of the P.N.I., ended up as the essential core of the local and regional National Committees.
25 Koesnodiprodjo, *Himpunan. 1945*, p. 46.

and it is probable also that there was opposition from leaders of pre-war political parties. But there are good grounds for suspecting that rivalries for control of it were more important. Still another answer may be that the K.N.I.P., inaugurated on August 29th, feared the P.N.I. as a rival and forced its suppression. The comment made by the President in his August 23rd speech (quoted above), to the effect that while the K.N.I.P. would be a temporary organization, the P.N.I. would be a permanent state institution, may support this interpretation.

On August 31st a national ministry was created under President Soekarno's leadership. Its membership was:[26]

Foreign Affairs	Mr. Subardjo
Interior	R. A, A. Wiranatakusuma
Justice	Prof. Mr. Dr. Supomo
Health	Dr. Buntaran Martoatmodjo
Education	Ki Hadjar Dewantoro
Information	Amir Sjarifuddin
Finance	Dr. Samsi Sastrawidagda
Social Affairs	Mr. Iwa Kusumasumantri
Economic Affairs	Ir. Surachman Tjokroadisurjo
Communications	Abikusno Tjokrosujoso
Public Works	Abikusno Tjokrosujoso

Dr. Amir, Wachid Hasjim, Mr. Sartono, Mr. Maramis and Oto Iskandardinata served as Ministers without Portfolio. Mr. Harmani served temporarily in the place of Wiranatakusuma, and Mr. Ali Sastroamidjojo in that of Amir Sjarifuddin, who had only just been released from a *Kempeitai* jail.[27] With the exception of Amir Sjarifuddin all these men had worked with the Japanese to some degree, and all were 'older generation.'

---

26 *Kabinet-Kabinet Republik Indonesia*, Kementerian Penerangan, Djakarta, 1955, p. 17. There was a theoretical Ministry of Defence, but as yet no Minister. On October 6th, the missing (dead) Supri-jadi who had led the tragic Blitar revolt was appointed to the post, On October 20th, Suljoadikusumo became Minister ad interim.

27 He had originally been sentenced to death for underground activities, but through the intercession of Soekarno and Hatta, this sentence was commuted to life imprisonment. See Pakpahan, *op. cit.*, pp. 97-99.

Many of them had in fact held almost identical posts under the Japanese Military Administration.

There is no reason to believe that the new Cabinet Ministers were not chosen with precisely this consideration in mind. One observer noted that:[28]

> "there is no reason to conceal the fact that although Ministers had been appointed by this time, there were still many of them who acted as Japanese officials, and so to speak had a dual role. On the one hand they were officials for the Japanese, who still exercised real power; on the other hand they were also appointed Ministers of the Indonesian Republic that had just been proclaimed."

Vice-President Hatta commented in a similar vein:[29]

> "The method we decided on was to seize power from within. Orders were issued to every government official to acknowledge himself as an official of the Republic of Indonesia, and ready to accept only orders given him by superiors of Indonesian nationality... Indonesian deputy-heads of departments were confirmed as official heads, taking their orders directly from the Government of the Republic of Indonesia... To hasten this seizure of power from within, the greater part of the Ministers of the first Presidential Cabinet were selected from those men who were already placed at the top of the departmental hierarchies as *Butjos* (Heads) or *Sanyos* (Advisors). In this way, the downward channels of command could be controlled, and the Japanese could easily be set aside."

Nishimura's perspective is illustrated by his description of Wiranatakusuma's activities in the Home Affairs Department:[30]

---

28 Nawawi Dusky, in *Harian Abadi*, August 22, 1955.
29 Hatta, "Isi Proklamasi" in *Fakta dan Dokumen2, Supplemen I*, p. 2.
30 *Statement* of Nishimura, April 25, 1947, p. 9. Apparently the Min-isters holding "new" portfolios (such as Foreign Affairs, Social Affairs, etc.) in the Cabinet, were also given appointments in the Japanese bureaucratic structure, the appointment being backdated to before the Japanese surrender, when the Japanese could still legally make appointments.

"He was of course responsible to the Gunseikan. True, the Indonesians may have liked to call him Minister of the Republic when he held this position. But after the Rangoon Agreement[31] we suspended all appointments of Indonesian officials."

This ambiguous dualistic role played by the Cabinet was useful for all parties, and provided a way for Japanese and Indonesians to avoid direct and open conflict. But it certainly did little to raise the credit of the Cabinet itself which was anyway in no position to take the initiative. Its survival depended largely on the broking function it performed, and it was bound to last only so long as all the parties to its formation continued to be satisfied with a slow and gradual change in the *status quo*. With the Allies about to land, and the *pemudas*' growing discontent with their marginal position under the new government, the Cabinet's prospects were not very good.

In the meantime, outside the conference rooms of Djakarta, the situation was developing rapidly. On August 18th, there was for the first time under the Occupation a daylight attack on a Police Headquarters. The incident took place in Serang.[32] The Japanese were seriously alarmed, the affair confirming all their forebodings. Nishimura and his staff decided that the Peta and *Heiho* and other para-military organizations had to be disarmed and demobilized immediately, not simply to satisfy the Allies, but to protect themselves. Considering the low state of Japanese morale at the time, this plan was carried out with astonishing coolness and considerable success. With a few exceptions, the Peta units were taken completely by surprise,[33] and seemed to be even more confused by the pace of events than the Japanese.[34] One story is that the military authorities summoned all Battalion and Company Commanders to Bogor.

---

31 The so-called Rangoon Agreement was the preliminary arrangement prior to the formal instrument of surrender of the Southern Territories. It was signed by representatives of Marshal Terauchi in the presence of the South East Asia Command at Rangoon on August 27, 1945. The formal instrument was not signed until September 12, in Singapore. Rajendra Singh, *op. cit.*, pp. 172f.

32 *Statement* of Nishimura, April 15, 1947, p. 2. Nishimura claimed there were 1, 100 Japanese casualties, including 700 killed.

33 There are reports that Hatta managed to get word out to Kasman Singodimedjo and Abdul Kadir, and as a result some arms were cached in Djakarta at least before the Japanese arrived.

34 Cf. Bachsan, *op. cit.*, pp. 63–65.

On arrival they were disarmed and interned. Secret orders were certainly issued to the Japanese NCOs attached to Peta units, to demobilize the troops in their charge, and collect their arms in central dumps where they could be more easily guarded, preferably in the Residency capitals, The execution of the operation, of course, varied from place to place. It should be remembered that the official announcement of the Japanese surrender was not made until August 21st, so that outside the larger cities there must have been many areas where Japanese military authority was still unquestioned. The Japanese Army astutely softened the blow of demobilization, and may have diverted natural, but awkward questions, by paying men 6 months' salary in advance, as well as a special advance "*Lebaran*" clothing bonus.³⁵ And, as Nishimura put it, "Luckily the rice-harvest that summer was the best in years."³⁶

When the news of the demobilization of the Peta and *Heiho* reached the Indonesian leaders, they were apparently at first non-plussed. But a series of so-called *Badan2 Keamanan Rakjat* (People's Security Corps) were set up on August 22nd, ostensibly only to stop looting and carry out certain other police functions. Soekarno was able to use his authority over the *Djawa Hookookai apparatus* to publicize the B.K.R. s and to provide them with organizational nuclei. According to one story, the initiative in this affair was taken by the acting head of the Internal Affairs Department, R.A.A. Wiranatakusuma. Another account has it that Urip Sumohardjo (who had held a unique position within the Dutch colonial army) and several ex-Peta officers came to Hatta and Soekarno shortly after the Proclamation urging the formation of a national army. The two political leaders felt that such a move would be premature, and so, after some days of hesitation, Soekarno told Urip that he had "been thinking the whole thing over very carefully — Indonesia's situation in the international world. We must immediately have some means of maintaining public security aside from the police, but not an army..."³⁷

---

35 *Statement* of Nishimura, April 15, 1947, p. 3.
36 *Ibid*. It may be recalled that there were about 70, 000 Japanese troops on Java at the time, as opposed to perhaps 50, 000 Peta-*Heiho*.
37 For an early public statement by Soekarno on the B.K.R. s, see his speech of August 23rd, "The Change of the Times and Our Duty," in *Fakta dan Dokumen2*, pp. 4-10, where he urged all ex-Peta and *Heiho* elements to unite their strength in the B.K.R. s. Be sure, he added, "the time will come when you will be called to become soldiers in the Indonesian National Army." Cf. also Nishijima,

Although in theory the B.K.R. s were to be co-ordinated and directed from Djakarta, they were from the beginning highly autonomous groups, locally oriented, with plans and ambitions of their own.[38] In some areas they were simply bands of villagers armed with bamboo spears and knives. In other areas, they tended to crystallize round ex-*Peta* and *Heiho* officers. On August 22nd, the Japanese began to release the Battalion and Company commanders they had interned during the demobilization operation, and these commanders immediately hurried back to their home training-grounds. In many cases they tried to re-assemble groups of demobilized members of the Peta, and active *pemuda* from the *Keibodan* and *Seinendan*.[39] However they faced strong competition from junior offi-cers who were as well educated and as capable as their superiors, and who were often closer to their men. The result was a rapid disintegration of the hierarchy of the Peta, as many Section Commanders, Platoon Commanders and even 'privates' broke away to form their own "*gerombolan*." These bands were held together less by formal discipline or military sub-ordination than by the charismatic qualities of the individual leader, who often heightened his authority by clothing it with political and magico-religious symbols.[40]

Meanwhile on Sumatra revolutionary activity was also beginning. The Japanese governor of Palembang, Miyake, testified that young "agitators" were sent over from Java immediately after the Proclamation to rouse the local population.[41] By August 19th, the situation was serious enough for a special Governors' Conference to be held at Bukittinggi. The conference agreed on an informal basis to put themselves completely under the military authority of the local division commanders, in order to ensure

---

Verklaring (Marine-Kantoor), March 25-29, 1947, pp. 1f. For Urip and Soekarno, see *Fakta dan Dokumen2*, pp. 87f.

38 Serious attempts to co-ordinate these local units into a national army probably date from the Government's establishment of the *Tentara Keamanan Rakjat* on October 5th. See Koesnodiprodjo, *Himpunan. 1945*, p. 54 for the proclamation of the T. K. R. and *ibid.*, p. 92 for further official amplification.

39 Cf. however Kahin, *op. cit.*, p. 137. See also Tjantrik Mataram, *op. cit.*, pp. 9f.

40 Cf. Taniguchi, *op. cit.*, pp. 537f.

41 *Statement* of Lt. Gen. Toshio Miyake, December 19, 1946, pp. 1f. Apparently the Sumatra high command enraged the 16th Army head quarters on Java by wiring them: "Situation in Java having grave and unfavorable influence on Sumatra's peace and order. Please control disturbing activities in your area. Take necessary steps to check infiltration of agitators from Java into Sumatra." Anonymous Japanese Officer, *Beschouwingen.*, June 21-23, 1947, p. 33.

cohesive action and prevent disturbances.[42]

By the last days of August, the initial daily expectation of the Allies' arrival had begun to wear off. The psychological advantage, which had up to now lain largely with Soekarno and Hatta, and to some extent with the Japanese, began to pass to other groups. President Soekarno appealed to "the people of Indonesia to be united as one whole at this present time, to stand behind the Leaders," avoiding "mutual accusations" and recriminations. He urged the formation of local National Committees (K. N. I.), who would devote all their energy and devotion to: 1) Announcing the will of the Indonesian people to live as a free Nation. 2) Uniting of all strata and occupations so that everywhere throughout Indonesia, the solidarity of complete and close national unity will be achieved. 3) Assisting in calming the people and participating in protecting public security. 4) Assisting the Leaders in putting the ideals of the Indonesian Nation into effect, and in the regions, helping the Local Governments to promote the well-being of the public. He concluded on this sober note:

> "To proclaim Independence is easy. To make a Constitution is not difficult. To elect a President and a Vice-President is easier still. But to form the bodies and the posts of authority and administration of the State, as well as to seek international recognition, especially under conditions such as the present, where the Japanese Government is still obliged by the international *status quo* to remain in this country to run the administration and maintain public order — these tasks are not easy!"[43]

The President's speech reflected a state of increasing tension and disorder in Java. Outside Djakarta, the B.K.R.'s and many other less official groupings were springing up overnight, and taking the initiative into their own hands. They attacked isolated Japanese encampments, broke into the concentration camps, raided ammunition dumps and arsenals, attacked local Chinese, and even struggled among themselves. All over Java there was fighting as Japanese and Indonesians tried to disarm

---

42 *Statement* of Miyake, December 19, 1946, *loc. cit.*
43 Speech of President Soekarno, "The Change of the Times and Our Duty," given on August 23, 1945, as cited in *Fakta dan Dokumen2*, pp. 4-10.

one another. In areas where the Japanese had behaved with cruelty, the tension was especially great. The Japanese were fearful of retribution, and the Indonesians determined to exact revenge. In some areas agreements made between the responsible local Indonesian authorities and the Japanese were broken by independent action on the part of *pemuda* elements or angry mobs, thus heightening mutual suspicion and hostility. Generally speaking the Japanese were loth to surrender their arms because to do so was to expose themselves completely to the mercy of the population, which for emotional and political reasons could not but be rather uncertain. On the one hand in Banjumas, where relations between the Japanese Resident Iwashige and his Indonesian deputy, Mr. Iskaq Tjokroadisurjo were excellent, an arrangement was made for the peaceable transfer of large quantities of military equipment to the local Peta Battalion Commander Sudirrnan, later to become Commander-in-Chief of the Republican Armies.[44] But the situation in Banjumas was the exception rather than the rule. The revolutionary tide was rising rapidly and almost uncontrollably. As Soekarno put it, "Indeed it is not easy to keep quiet and calm in a time like this, in a time when changes come as suddenly as the sky falling to the earth."[45]

The already grave difficulties faced by the Japanese were compounded by the instructions remitted to them by the Allies. The South East Asia Command had issued orders that all armaments were to be collected together at certain specified places, and guarded till the Allied detachments arrived to assume control. All Japanese troops were to be disarmed except for five rifle cartridges, and grouped at relocation camps, which would eventually become evacuation centres. At the same time, the requirement that essential services be maintained, the administrative apparatus be kept in operation, and law and order preserved, presented an overwhelming task for the deeply demoralized Japanese Army.[46] Their problems were

---

44 Gandasubrata, *op. cit.*, pp. 9, 19. Sudirman was actually the Battalion Commander in Kroja. He had been a teacher in the *Muhammadijah* movement before the war. As customary with Peta Battalion Comman-ders, he held a political post in the civilian administration, as head of the local *Sendenka* (branch of the Department of Propaganda).
45 Soekarno, "The Change of the Times and Our Duty," in *Fakta dan Dokumen2*, p. 4.
46 Cf. "*Orders for Japanese Surrender*", August 18, 1945, as cited above at footnote 280. See also *Statement* of Nishimura, April 10, 1947, pp. 4, 6; *Statement* of Nishimura, April 25, 1947, p. 4; Anonymous Japanese Officer, *Beschouwingen...*, June 21-23, 1947, pp 8f., comments on the increasing difficulty of the 16th Army's high command getting its orders obeyed by local units;

made no easier by an incautious broadcast from Singapore to the effect that "the Allies have no intention of disarming the Indonesian police or Soekarno's bodyguards."[47] This allowed the *pemudas* to claim Allied approval when they demanded and/or seized Japanese arms. The gradual transfer of military supplies and personnel into the interior where the Allied-designated relocation camps were situated made the coastal region particularly dangerous for isolated and straggling Japanese units. Maeda recalled later that some 80 Japanese soldiers were cut down in the Bekasi area.[48] And this was only one in a series of such confrontations and massacres,

In spite of Yamamoto's efforts to discipline his forces by repeatedly assuring them that the surrender had been on the Emperor's personal order,[49] and warning them of their duty not to hurt Japan's cause before the victorious Allies, desertions increased, communications in Java became increasingly disrupted and haphazard,[50] and the imposing structure of the Japanese administration began to disintegrate, One Japanese observer noted that:[51]

> "Japanese Army Headquarters was busy receiving detailed reports of the complete surrender of Japan coming in successively each day. The Military Government offices lost their function. Japanese administrators, with no instructions to receive, transferred the administration to Indonesian officials each according to their judgment, and started to prepare themselves for reaching the internment camps in the inland areas."

It can safely be said that by the beginning of September with the mounting difficulties of the Japanese, the unobtrusive but steady erosion of their bureaucratic authority,[52] the growing confidence of the older leaders and

---

Nishijima, *Verklaring (Marine-Kantoor)*, March 25-29, 1947, pp. 1-3.
47 As reported by Anonymous Japanese Officer, *Beschouwingen.*, June 21-23, 1947, p. 35.
48 As cited in Aziz, *op. cit.* p. 253.
49 Nishijima, *Verklaring (Marine-Kantoor)*, March 25-29, 1947, p. 2.
50 As noted above, the Allies forbade the use of radio to the Japanese Army.
51 Taniguchi, *op. cit.*, p. 537.
52 *Statement* of Nishimura, April 10, 1947, p. 6. Nishimura notes that Indonesian officials simply began withholding information, and thus isolating their Japanese 'superiors.' See also *Statement* of Nishimura, April 25, 1947, p. 9. Here Nishimura comments that though the Japanese officials

the surge of revolutionary fervour among the younger generation, a new atmosphere had developed on Java. The tide now ran heavily in favour of the Indonesians, who were becoming increasingly well-organized and united. Hatta claimed that by this time "the Japanese were no longer permitted to enter government offices. In areas outside Djakarta, they were arrested or confined to their homes."[53] In many rural districts where there were few Japanese, local K.N.I. had already assumed wide authority.

It was also early in September that the first signs of Allied activity became directly visible. The R.A.P.W.I. (Recovery of Allied Prisoners of War and other Internees) organization landed some agents to bring emergency medical aid to Allied P.O.W. and others in immediate need.[54] The Indonesians did their best to co-operate with this group. Then on September 15th, Rear-Admiral Patterson of the 5th Royal Cruiser Squadron, accompanied by Dr. Charles van der Plas, the NICA representative, sailed into Tandjung Priok on H.M.S. Cumberland.[55] Patterson immediately began to try to reconnoitre the local situation, and consulted the Japanese high command first of all. The unanimous testimony from the Japanese side warned the Allies of the tremendous degree of political excitement that prevailed on Java. Yamamoto urged the Allied Commander to allow all Indonesian officials to retain the posts they now held, and to make a clear policy statement about the extent of political participation that the Allies were prepared to permit. He said that though rivalries did exist between Nationalists, Islamic elements and professional administrators, they were all solidly behind independence. Particular tact should be exercised on the matter of the Indonesian flag and national anthem, because in the present context, any real or imagined insults would result in massive sabotage, strikes and possibly even the murder of prisoners massed in the hinterland.[56] When Dr. van

---

tried to stick together, they were elbowed aside and even threatened by the increasingly truculent Indonesians.
53 Hatta, "Isi Proklamasi," in *Fakta dan Dokumen2, Supplemen I*, p. 2.
54 Cf. e. g. Rajendra Singh, *op. cit.*, p. 179.
55 Donnison, *op. cit.*, p. 423f. An advance group of British intelligence officers had previously been parachuted into Java on September 8th. In Rajendra Singh's account (see Rajendra Singh, *op. cit.*, p. 222), Patterson did not arrive till the 16th, and the Cumberland was accompanied by the Dutch cruiser Tromp.
56 *Letter of General Yamamoto to Rear-Admiral Patterson of September* 23, 1945, entitled "An

der Plas criticized the Japanese for allowing "terrorists" to intimidate the population into obeying their orders, the former Gunseikan told Patterson that if the Indonesians thought that the Allies would help them towards Independence, they would be only too glad to co-operate. He warned the British not to treat Soekarno and Hatta as war-criminals. They had co-operated with the Japanese simply to protect their countrymen, and advance the cause of Indonesian freedom.[57]

Van der Plas, however, as the representative of NICA, was in no position to accept the situation.[58] Pointing to the recently signed Anglo-Dutch agreement of August 24th, he rejected the idea of accepting the mediation and help of the Indonesians in repatriating prisoners of war and maintaining law and order. But for the moment he had no alternative. No Allied troops had as yet arrived.[59] Patterson reported to headquarters that there was no possibility of re-occupying Java as a whole. The best the Allies could do, he said, would be to occupy key enclaves on the coast, and accept the co-operation offered by the Indonesian regime in evacuating Japanese soldiers and Allied internees. If the Dutch wanted to extend their authority outside these areas, they would have to try to do it themselves. The Allies (i. e. the British) simply did not have the troops available to carry out the original plans agreed on before the Japanese surrender, which had been made without any real understanding of the political situation in Java. On September 28th, Lord Mountbatten accepted the Admiral's recommendations, and reversed his earlier instructions that the Indonesian Republic should be given no sort of recognition.[60] General

---

Individual Opinion which may interest the Allied Powers with regard to the future management of Indonesia," pp. 1-3.

57 *Summary* of a meeting between General Yamamoto, Admiral Patterson and Dr. van der Plas on board H.M.S. Cumberland, September 21, 1945, p. 1.

58 Dr. van der Plas, in the view of American intelligence the most favourably inclined of the Dutch policy-makers towards the views of the Indonesian political elite, summarized his views on Indonesia's future with the phrase: "We Dutch and Indonesians must develop a nation oriental in its culture and art and Western in its democratic ideals." See U.S. Office of Strategic Services, Research and Analysis Branch, *Report # 28769*, "Dutch Attitudes towards the Future of the Netherlands East Indies," February 2, 1945. According to Donnison, op. cit., p. 425, the Dutch were convinced that once a few "extremists" had been removed from the scene, they would have no difficulty in winning over the "moderates" and the peasants.

59 According to Donnison, *ibid.*, 7 companies of the Royal Dutch Colonial Army were poised to leave for Indonesia, and 6 brigades of top-flight Dutch troops were ready to embark in Holland at this time.

60 Cf. Donnison, *ibid.*; also Rajendra Singh, *op. cit.*, p. 223. The Dutch were naturally very angry.

Christison, newly appointed Allied Commander in the area, announced, before leaving for Djakarta, that "the Indonesian Government will not be expelled and will be expected to continue civil administration in the areas outside those occupied by British forces".[61] There was no question of an All-Java Allied Military Administration.

Meanwhile the *pemudas* had set up their own grass-roots centre of operations at Menteng 31, and began to issue their own propaganda and 'program.' The key figures in the organization appear to have been Soekarni, Maruto Nitimihardjo, Adam Malik, Wikana, Chaerul Saleh, Panduwiguna, Kusnaeni, Darwis, Djohar Noer, Armunanto and Hanafi.[62] Its five-point manifesto was as follows:[63]

1. The Unitary State of the Republic of Indonesia came into being on August 17, 1945, and the People are now independent, free of Foreign rule.
2. All power must be placed in the hands of the State and People of Indonesia.
3. Japan is now defeated, and has no more right to exercise authority over Indonesian territory.
4. The People of Indonesia must seize arms from the hands of the Japanese.
5. All enterprises (offices, factories, mines, plantations, etc.) must be seized from the Japanese, and controlled by the Indonesian People (especially by the Workers).

Under a Central Action Committee several subordinate units were set up: the *Angkatan Pemuda Indonesia* (A.P.I. — Indonesian Youth Corps), as an armed para-military brigade, *Barisan Rakjat Indonesia* (Indonesian People's Front), as a peasant organization, and *Barisan Buruh Indonesia* (Indonesian Labour Front), as a labour action group.

Partly out of impatience at the cautious Fabian tactics of the Cabinet which they regarded as still trying to accomodate the Japanese as far as possible, partly perhaps to undercut the Dutch, who were broadcasting

---
61 Cf. Rajendra Singh, op. cit., p. 224, citing P. Gerbrandy, *Indonesia*, p. 99.
62 Malik, *op. cit.*, p. 69. Sjahrir was probably also involved indirectly.
63 Malik, *ibid.*, pp. 69f.

that those who had collaborated with the Japanese would be treated as war-criminals, the Central Action Committee called for a drastic "grassroots" assumption of power. Under its leadership a series of local actions such as the seizure of the Djakarta railroad system by the railroad workers, and similar expropriations of plantations, were rapidly carried out.[64] The intention of the Action Committee seems to have been to use these faits accomplis by anonymous groups with anonymous leaders, to in-crease the radical temper of the masses, ensure a 'leftist' and popular counterpoise to the Cabinet and the older politicians, and to parry Allied charges that Indonesia was being run by a 'Japanese-made' government. As word spread of the Committee's activities, the example of the Djakarta *pemudas* was rapidly imitated by youth groups in other cities on Java, somewhat to the embarrassment of the older leaders, who were trying to establish coherent lines of authority from the top downward.[65]

The psychological climax to the struggle between the Indonesians and Japanese was the "incident" of September 19th. According to Tan Malakka, this occurred as a result of his own idea that the Indonesians in Djakarta should put on a massive popular demonstration of Indonesian unity and determination not to submit to Japanese control any longer.[66] Malik asserts that the plan for a mass demonstration originated with the Action Committee.[67] Tan Malakka further avers that a majority of the Cabinet, and especially Iwa Kusumasumantri and Subardjo, accepted the idea and agreed to carry it out. Careful plans were then laid for a gigantic rally on the Koningsplein (Ikada), When word reached the Japanese of the plans, they forbade the Cabinet to proceed, and told Soekarno and Hatta

---

64 For details, see Malik, *ibid.*, pp. 69-73; also Nishijima, Kishi, *etal.*, *op. cit.*, p. 515.
65 It was perhaps in answer to *pemuda* agitation, that Vice-President Hatta, in a radio speech on August 29th, said: "But aside from being ready to die, the youth must also be ready to live to struggle together with the common people for the accomplishment of the ideals of the Indonesian Republic, based on the sovereignty of the people... The youth that come from the common people already bear within them the people's spirit. Only their political consciousness must be deepened. But for the educated youth. it is necessary to have training and instruction in how to bring themselves close to the people's heart. *There is no better training and instruction than disciplining themselves to follow the popular will.... The youth must not act alone,* failing to bind themselves to the people, and outside the main movement of the people..." *Fakta dan Dokumen2*, p. 69. The italics are the writer's. It is clear that there were grave differences between Hatta's and the *pemudas*' ideas of the content of the people's will.
66 Tan Malakka, *op. cit.*, p. 61.
67 Malik, *op. cit.*, p. 74.

that they would be held personally responsible for any trouble that might arise. In the face of the Japanese threat Soekarno, Hatta and Supomo came out against holding the rally, while Iwa, Subardjo, Ki Hadjar Dewantoro, Mr. Gatot and Abikusno favored it.

Tan Malakka reports that finding themselves in a minority, Soekarno and Hatta sent in their resignations to the Japanese(!). However when the Japanese requested them to continue in office they agreed to withdraw their resignations. At the same time President Soekarno, in his capacity as Commander-in-Chief still banned any demonstrations.
However, led by Adam Malik, then a Vice-Chairman of the K.N.I.P., and Abikusno, the *pemudas* refused to obey, and a crowd of 200, 000 was assembled under their leadership in the Koningsplein.[68]

There are at least two fairly good reasons for not accepting this story entirely at its face value. It is hard to imagine what 'Japanese' offices Soekarno and Hatta could resign from, or if Tan Malakka is talking about the Presidency and Vice-Presidency, why Soekarno and Hatta should have offered to resign from offices of which the Japanese took no legal cognizance anyway. Secondly, as yet no national army had been created, so there are difficulties in understanding how Soekarno, in his capacity as Commander-in-Chief, could have banned anything (especially with the Japanese still in military control). The truth of the matter probably is that Soekarno and Hatta, realizing that they were indispensable to the Japanese, as instruments for controlling *pemuda* activism, were able to put very strong pressure on them to agree to the meeting taking place, while assuming responsibility for the consequences. The threat of withdrawing from their mediating role must have commanded the respect of the Japanese at this stage. Though the initiative for the meeting may have come from *pemuda* groups, the two leaders were able to turn it to their own advantage.

Adam Malik's story is not only more convincing than Tan Malakka's, but corroborates this interpretation and fills in another side of the picture. He writes that the threat of resignation was sent to Menteng 31 and was designed to pressure the *pemudas* into cancelling their preparations for the meeting. The Menteng 31 group then sent Adam Malik, third Vice-Chairman of the K.N.I.P., to try to persuade the Cabinet to change its stand.

---

68 Tan Malakka, *op. cit.*, pp. 62f.

He was able to convince Soekarno and Hatta that popular expectations had reached a point where serious outbreaks might be expected if the rally was cancelled. A message was then sent to the Japanese authorities saying that the meeting would be held and that "the Republic" would be responsible for the consequences.[69]

Tension in Djakarta mounted as the Japanese sent tanks and machine-gun squads to cover all entrances to the Koningsplein. The *pemudas* who were leading the huge crowds of workers, peasants from outside Djakarta, and other mass elements, were reportedly armed only with sharpened bamboo spears. But their numbers and their determination were such that the Japanese did not dare to start firing. The crisis was finally resolved only when Soekarno appeared, and with great skill calmed the crowd down and sent them quietly back to their homes.[70] The *Kernpeitai* immediately retaliated against the Action Committee. That night the *pemuda* headquarters at *Menteng 31* were ransacked. Darwis, Sidik, Hanafi, Aidit, A. Manafroni, Wahidin and Lukman were arrested and taken first to the *Kempeitai* headquarters and later to the Special Prison at Bukitduri. Malik was arrested two days later. But the Japanese riposte was basically ineffective. The flow of radical nationalist propaganda was barely checked. Popular feeling was aroused by the arrests.[71] More important still, Soekarno's demonstration of his enormous spiritual authority on this occasion was a crucial psychological turning-point. From September 19th onwards, the Indonesians assumed a full spiritual ascendancy over their adversaries.

The other important political development of this period was the obscure political manoeuvring between the rival organizations of Sjahrir and Tan Malakka. However inasmuch as this struggle has been fully analyzed elsewhere,[72] and in fact came to a head only in the period after that covered by this study, a brief sketch will perhaps suffice. Sjahrir

---

69 Malik, *op. cit.*, p. 75. "The Republic" in this context refers in general to the Cabinet and in particular, presumably, to Soekarno and Hatta.
70 For a paraphrased excerpt from Soekarno's speech, see Malik, *ibid.*, p. 76. Otherwise, see Tan Malakka, *op. cit.*, p. 63, and, for a less lurid account, Kahin, *op. cit.*, p. 137, though the date given there, August 19th, is a month too early. For a highly atmospheric photograph of the occasion, see *Lukisan Revolusi, 1945-1949*, Kementerian Penerangan, Jogjakarta, 1949, p. 59.
71 Malik, *op. cit.*, pp. 77f.
72 See Kahin, *op. cit*, pp. 147-192.

had been very unwilling to endorse the Republican Government in the first three weeks after independence. His general attitude was that the Government represented, in too many cases, people who had actively collaborated with the Japanese, and had become affected with Japanese or Fascist ideology.[73] However a journey that he made through Java in late August and early September convinced him that Soekarno was essential to the revolutionary struggle, and more important still, that there was enough popular support for a successful resistance to the Dutch. Though he refused a possibly *pro forma* offer of a Cabinet post by President Soekarno, he agreed to support the regime.[74] And during a crucial period in which it appears that Tan Malakka was aiming to supplant Soekarno as the head of the revolutionary movement, Sjahrir threw his support to Soekarno, and succeeded in heading off his rival's bid for supreme power[75]

At the same time the remnants of the *Kaigun* organization[76] continued with their plans for assisting the Revolution through the trans-fer of weapons, ammunition, and other military equipment into Nationalist hands.[77] It is reported that both Nishijima and Yoshizumi joined the Nationalist movement personally and that Yoshizumi was killed fighting for the Revolution.[78] Maeda was arrested by the British in October 1945 on the grounds that some 3, 000 Japanese had deserted into the interior while under his charge.[79] In Surabaja, Admiral Shibata adroitly delivered almost the entire contents of the Naval Headquarters' arsenal in that city to the *pemudas*.[80] And according to one story at least, it was Nishijima

---

73 Cf. e. g. his controversial book, *Perdjoeangan Kita* (Our Struggle), Pertjetakan Repoeblik Indonesia, Djakarta, 1945, *passim*.
74 Kahin, *op. cit.*, p. 147. For a version more hostile to Sjahrir, see Nishijima, Kishi *et al*, *op. cit.*, p. 516.
75 Kahin, *op. cit.*, pp. 149-151.
76 Kahin, *op. cit.*, p. 136, says that Maeda was jailed by the Army immediately alter independence, but not for how long.
77 For some light on this, see Anonymous Japanese Officer, *Beschouwingen...*, June 21 -23, 1947, p 20, and E. B. VanHulten, *Rapport...* July 24, 1946, pp. 8f.
78 Apparently in East Java in 1948, after helping to build an Army division. Cf. also E. B. VanHulten, *Rapport...*, July 24, 1946, p. 8; Anonymous Japanese Officer, *Beschouwingen...*, June 21-23, 1947, p. 20.
79 E. B. VanHulten, *ibid.*, p. 9, Cf. Nishijima, *Verklaring...*, March 10-13, 1947, pp. 10-12, for a very contrasting version. Also see Anonymous Japanese Officer, *ibid.*, p. 9.
80 See E. B. VanHulten, *ibid.*, p 8; Anonymous Japanese Officer, *ibid.*, p. 25, Cf. also the suavely bland report given by Admiral Shibata to the Allies, He describes how in spite of all his "pleas

who, with Jusuf Hasan, Sutomo, Djojo-pranoto and the K.R.I.S. leader Evart Lankay, organized the tremendous Indonesian resistance to the British forces at the Battle of Surabaja in November 1945.[81]

On September 29th, the first British troops arrived in Djakarta, and once again the political kaleidoscope in Indonesia was given a shake. But the new patterns that emerged are beyond the scope of this study. For with the arrival of the Allied Forces, the Japanese Occupation had come to an end.

---

that our arms should be given straight to the Allies," the Indonesians seized the Naval Arsenal at Surabaja. The Japanese fought for one and a half hours, but then Shibata acceded to Indonesian demands "in order to save lives." *Report of the Commander-in-Chief, 2nd South Seas Fleet to HQ Allied Administration, Batavia*, October 3, 1945, pp. 1f. Reportedly the *pemudas* used the Naval equipment to help break into and seize the Army Headquarters' ammunition depot in Surabaja.

81 E. B. VanHulten, *ibid.*, p. 5. Together they formed the *Persatuan Rak-jat Djelata*, which helped direct the resistance in the city.

www.ingramcontent.com/pod-product-compliance
Lightning Source LLC
Chambersburg PA
CBHW020742230426
43665CB00009B/522